"Unmasked gives Ame
progressives take charg
every way imaginable. C
rats. The free spirit of Colorado is no match for the tyranny that has ensued and until we stop them from imposing their destructive and overreaching policies into every state, we can forget what a free America look like."

—Jon Caldara

"Unmasked 2020 tells the complete story of how progressives yanked Colorado to the Left – from dominating its media to shutting down energy options. But it also points out how their excesses are catching up with them, and how a real "fight back" effort can restore common sense and balance."

—John Fund

"This book is a dynamite blast aimed at Colorado elites whose smugness and complacency are ill-suited to meeting the formidable challenge we now face to the very foundations of our constitutional liberties."

— Mark Hillman

"There is a destructive movement on the march in America, which is bent on destroying everything we hold dear. The violence in the streets would not be possible without the active collusion of the Democrat Party whose elected officials support its agendas. These goals are laid bare in UNMASKED, which is a noble attempt to save this beautiful state."

— David Horowitz

"I guarantee Governor Polis and his media cheerleaders will not like this book, an eye-opening chronicle of Colorado's radical Democrats' costly mismanagement of the Wuhan Virus pandemic and the budget crisis his foolish shutdown triggered."

— Michelle Malkin

"Given the lurch to the left by Colorado Democrats, this book is timely and important during this 2020 election and beyond. The Democratic Party of Roy Romer and Dick Lamm is dead and buried."

— Dick Wadhams

UNMASKED2020

Colorado's Radical Left Turn
and a
Warning to America

Edited by
Charles Heatherly
Kevin Lundberg

Cover Design by Clockwise Media Group
Photographs by Kevin Lundberg

Published by
The Republican Study Committee
of Colorado

ISBN: 978-0-578-74801-6

DEDICATED TO OUR FRIEND AND PATRIOT

RUSH LIMBAUGH

Winner of Presidential Medal of Freedom
February 2020

ACKNOWLEDGMENTS

The idea for this book originated in April and May of 2020 in conversations one of the co-editors had with staff and lawmakers of the Colorado General Assembly's House of Representatives during the unprecedented, fear-induced ten-week "pandemic recess." To abuse Charles Dickens' *Tale of Two Cities,* the 2020 legislative session was indeed the worst of times but nowhere near the best of times. The noxious smell of executive hubris seeped upward from Governor Polis' first floor office into the deliberative chambers above.

In early June the two principal architects and co-editors of the book, Charles Heatherly and Kevin Lundberg, began jointly recruiting a baker's dozen contributors; together they planned the scope, purpose, timetable and funding needed to publish and promote the volume. In June, the board of directors of the Republican Study Committee of Colorado, the conservative caucus in the legislature, led by chair Representative Perry Buck and 2021 chair-elect Senator Rob Woodward, approved RSCC's official sponsorship of the book.

As the plan evolved and a schedule of tasks and benchmarks was adopted, grassroots leaders Patricia Kurgan and Jan Cook joined the project and contributed immensely, not only in time but sound advice and encouragement. Carol Kirkstadt provided wise counsel and volunteered weeks and long hours of professional assistance in formatting the edited chapters and related material, based on her personal experience in self-publication of several books.

The most important acknowledgment must be to the book's coauthors themselves, among them six current and former legislators. When approached, not one contributor declined to participate. No one said, "No, it can't be done." The support and encouragement of former State Senate President John Andrews was especially important throughout. Each of the authors agreed to deliver a manuscript on a specific topic, on a very tight timetable, and without a promise or certainty of compensation. The sponsors and editors also gratefully acknowledge the assistance of the Independence Institute and particularly Tracy Kimball Smith, the Institute's liaison with the innovative crowd-funding program, Freedomfy.com.

Finally, the book would not have seen the light of day without the financial support of over 200 individual donors, Coloradans all, citizen-patriots who believe with Ronald Reagan that America's best days are yet to come. In all likelihood, many of those donors remember Reagan's most important speech, "A Time for Choosing", delivered six years before his own successful presidential campaign, on the eve of the most devastating Republican Electoral College loss of the 20th Century. In a world where the enemies of liberty are *always* "full of passionate intensity," it is always "a time for choosing." In 2020, it's true as never before.

We acknowledge with deep gratitude the inspiration of patriots, crusaders and statesmen who, in peace and war, have helped guide the Party of Lincoln through many periods of danger and turmoil. May Providence continue to shine its light on our troubled nation!

The Republican Study Committee of Colorado
September 2020

CONTENTS

FOREWORD

UNMASKED2020 is a collection of commentaries on the government's executive and legislative actions during the historic 2020 session of the Colorado General Assembly. The 2019 legislative session had produced much equally radical legislation, like the knee-capping of the oil and gas industry in Senate Bill 181, but the 2020 session was more dramatic and arrogant in the rapid acceleration of Progressives' radical agenda. This occurred through an unprecedented confluence of events:

- the arrival in March of the malevolent Wuhan virus and the resulting declaration of a public health emergency by the governor;
- the cataclysmic economic meltdown stemming from Governor Polis's shut-down orders in response to the pandemic;
- the ten-week legislative recess, pushing the normal 120-day session into mid-June;
- the severe multi-year budget crisis resulting from the Governor's shutdown orders; and
- nightly riots on the Capitol grounds, continuing for weeks and affecting the work hours, the safety of legislators and employees, and not-so-subtly influencing the legislative agenda.

When reading the contributions offered by the authors, two things need to be kept in mind.

- First, the book is an anthology: each individual chapter presents the views and judgments of the specific author on the subjects and controversies discussed in that chapter. The fifteen authors do not necessarily agree with all of the views presented by the other contributors.
- The book is not a policy manifesto, and it does not attempt to cover every aspect of the 2020 session of the legislature. Authors evaluate several major actions which are characteristic of the session and will have serious impacts on Coloradans' lives and liberties for decades.

What the book does attempt to do is sound a wakeup call. By "unmasking" the deeply troublesome radicalism and dishonesty behind a media-driven narrative that misleads the citizenry, the authors hope to interrupt and help reverse Colorado's downhill rush to a California-style apocalypse.

Time is short to halt Colorado's slide into a civic chaos where the "Rule of Law" is no longer respected.

The Editors

INTRODUCTION: COLORADO'S RADICAL LEFT TURN AND A THREAT TO AMERICA

BY JOHN ANDREWS
Former Colorado Senate President

How do a free people lose their freedom? More often by inches than by miles. More often by neglect and passivity than by conscious consent or a losing fight.

It was said that Britain acquired its empire in a fit of absent-mindedness. Could a state like Colorado discard its proud tradition of liberty and limited government in much the same way?

And if this could happen in my state, couldn't it happen just as easily in any state?

Across the map, in states both blue and red, opportunistic leftists are primed to let no crisis go to waste. This book is our effort to alert Coloradans to what has overtaken them, and to warn our fellow Americans everywhere.

The book is a chronicle of lawmaking and lawbreaking, public attitudes and media narratives, in Colorado during the first eight months of 2020, one of the stormiest years our country has experienced since the Great Depression and World War II.

Of course, eight months is just the blink of an eye in the Centennial State's century and a half of history. Our contributors are not saying everything changed completely or irreversibly for Coloradans during that short time. But, we thought it important to lay down a record of how much *did* change, why that took place, and how it may alter our way of life in years to come—not for the better.

Turning the page into 2020 last January, Colorado was enjoying a robust economy, visitors from around the world were looking forward to winter vacations here, and it was expected the state's Democrat-dominated executive and legislative branches would move cautiously, as election-year wisdom dictates.

Compounding Crises

By March, only a few weeks later, this had all changed with the suddenness and vehemence of a "bomb cyclone" weather event. First, the coronavirus pandemic upended everything. Then in May, after another few weeks, racial tensions flared following the George Floyd death. Before long, well-organized seditious elements began abusing the people's freedom of assembly with violent, nihilist riots.

The shock and strain these compounding crises placed upon Colorado's institutions of self-government, and on the elected officials leading them, can hardly be overstated. Having run for governor and served in legislative leadership,

I don't envy the difficult judgment calls that Gov. Jared Polis, Senate President Leroy Garcia, and House Speaker KC Becker, decent individuals all, had to make.

But I agree with our chapter authors that these leaders and too many others in state government, local government, public health, and law enforcement did not rise to the occasion as we the people had a right to expect they should.

Nor did many of our news media, many of our judges, many of our educators, many of our churches. Across the ranks of our state's leadership elites, it must sadly be said that 2020 has not been their finest hour.

Not exempt from scrutiny, I hasten to add — as we seek to learn lessons and regain our balance — are some of the interests I've allied with as a conservative Republican. It's fair to ask how well GOP political leaders and business lobby groups and policy think tanks have met the moment. My tentative answer, between friends, is — probably not as well as they might have.

Today, as the state and nation are less than two months away from a bitterly contested, highly consequential election, Coloradans look around them and see this place we love sharply changed in ways that deeply worry many of us.

We see the governorship engorged with habit-forming powers to rule by edict. We see the General Assembly acquiring a taste for improvisational lawmaking and rule-bending. We see the courts imposing few checks on all this overreach. How much longer will the Colorado constitution be worth the paper it's written on?

We see the state's once-roaring economy reeling from

dubiously necessary shutdowns, with the timeline for recovery anyone's guess. Kids back in classrooms, fans back in stadiums, diners back in restaurants? Eventually, sure — but what's the damage toll until then?

We see the State Capitol itself, seat and symbol of our representative republican form of government, battered and defaced by hateful mobs. Graffiti scrubbed off, monument from the war to end slavery restored, the People's House again cherished and protected? Someday, maybe — but what's the hurry?

Danger of Faction

How much of this would have occurred no matter which party and what personalities were in power? How much of it was by design from the left — and merely the opening phase of a grander design set to unfold methodically year by year?

How much of the harm already done can be undone by countervailing electoral gains this fall and in upcoming election cycles? Many of us on the right fear that won't be easy.

Progressives' shrewdly constructed political and media infrastructure in Colorado was already showing its "ratchet power" to lock in one-way change when Adam Schrager and Rob Witwer published *TheBlueprint* in 2010. The ratchet has tightened since then, with one of its architects and financiers, multimillionaire Jared Polis, now sitting in the governor's office.

Arguably, the Colorado Democratic Party with its phalanx of outrider groups and its legion of megadonors has now become a classic instance of "faction," that bane of republics about which James Madison warns in *Federalist 10*.

A faction, Madison explains, is a political bloc so welded by self-interest that it no longer defers to constitutional restraints, a respect for the outnumbered opposition, a spirit of fair play, ethical norms, or even a sense of the common good.

Where faction prevails, he writes, "instability, injustice, and confusion" are rampant. Raw majoritarianism runs unchecked, and might makes right. If that sounds like what our state has lived through in 2020, we have a problem, Colorado.

Political Biopsy

We have, if you will, a raging illness in the body politic. The essays collected here are thus a sort of *biopsy*, a clinical analysis of samples from the diseased entity, aimed at finding out what's wrong and beginning to identify remedies.

But make no mistake. As troubled as things are, our state is far from needing an *autopsy*. Coloradans are a resilient and resourceful people. Freedom is in our DNA; so is justice, so are generosity and compassion. It would take a lot more adversity than 2020 has so far delivered to defeat us.

So we of the *UNMASKED2020* analytical team are energized with determination and hope in submitting these biopsy results for consideration and perhaps, in due course, for action. We believe Colorado's best days are still ahead — as are those of the USA.

In my early days as a state senator, two decades ago, it was funny to have constituents who should know better than to ask how I liked "being in Congress" and whether I could get them White House tour tickets. "Don't feel bad," I would joke when they apologized, "a hazy knowledge of state government is a sign of good mental health."

But in our new era of strongman governors and strident federalism, that's no longer the case. These days, neighbor, to paraphrase Lenin, state government is very interested — perhaps too much so — in you, whether or not you're interested in it.

We offer *UNMASKED2020* as a survival manual for liberty-loving neighbors from Denver to Dover to Del Mar and everywhere else nationwide. We second what Jon Caldara of the Independence Institute said to the authors of *The Blueprint*: "Colorado is big enough to be important but small enough that just a few people can radically change the political landscape."

True then and truer still today. Radical change on steroids has now overtaken our state — and it may be coming soon to yours. Be warned, America.

Part One:
2020: A Pandemic of Hubris

Do not steal.
Do not lie.
Do not deceive one another.

Leviticus 19:11

Test all things;
hold fast that which is good.

1 Thessalonians 5:21

1

STORM CLOUDS: THE TRUE RADICALISM OF THE 2019 SESSION

BY KEVIN LUNDBERG
Former Colorado State Senator

After 120 days, 598 bills, 32 billion dollars, and who knows how many votes and amendments, the 2019 session finally ended. It will take years to unravel all the fundamental changes that were forced on the people of Colorado in the first legislative session with Jared Polis as governor and his party in firm control of both houses of the legislature.

Political veterans shook their heads in disbelief. No one had ever seen so much damage done to our economy, our schools, parental authority, and specific industries (oil and gas, electric utilities, the rental industry, etc.), and commonly accepted cultural values (sex-education standards, identifying people as male or female in schools, on drivers' licenses, and on birth certificates).

These fundamental changes to Colorado form a complex web. Hopefully this chapter will help the reader more fully understand how significant these changes are for the people of Colorado, and how this began a process of unraveling the values and policies that have served our state well for many decades.

The 2019 session began a snowball that became an avalanche of radical left policies in 2020.

In this chapter, bills and other policies are divided into major topics and, as many bills overlap topics, they may be mentioned more than once.

Education and Parental Authority

We start here because this was the Governor's top priority. He and his supporters touted the creation of the all-day daycare, uh . . . kindergarten, as their greatest accomplishment (HB-1262). Right after the session, ads popped up on the radio saying this bill would save some families up to $400 a month, help parents get back to work, and help, "all kids have a better tomorrow."

These ads focused heavily on the daycare aspect of the plan. They promoted the fact that mom and dad can now get back to work sooner. The bill was not for the children. It was a law to get mom and dad out of the child's life as soon as possible. Secondly, this early start to the child's education should be seen in the context of other bills that set the tone for what public education means in Colorado. This includes the intersex bill (HB-1032), the intersectionality bill (HB-1192), the 12-year-old mental health bill (HB-1120), the immersion therapy bill (HB-1262), the bill to put a mental health worker in every grade of every school (HB-1017), and the bill to force all parents to register with the health department for immunization exemptions (HB-1312), which was killed by the Senate in 2019, but passed in 2020 as SB-163.

Let's get to the "free" part. HB-1262 may have translated into a free daycare for some parents, but it did so at an initial cost of between $175,000,000 — $185,000,000 to the state taxpayers. Furthermore, what is not accounted for in this gargantuan price tag is the additional classrooms that local districts must now find or build. This budget-busting bill is now a part of the fiscal crisis in Colorado's state budget.

Rally in Opposition to HB19-1032

HB-1032 was a radical rewrite of the state's policies on sex education in public schools. At its core, this bill is intended to normalize and teach the acceptance of (quoting from the bill) "INTERSEX INDIVIDUALS OR LESBIAN, GAY, BISEXUAL, OR TRANSGENDER INDIVIDUALS." I am in no way advocating intolerance for any individuals, but strongly question setting up a new normal, where the abnormal becomes the advocated value, and all are required to agree it is normal and desirable. There is no mention of teaching school children about the virtues of keeping sexual activity within the bounds of a married relationship. In fact, HB-1032 specifically says that abstinence cannot be taught as the primary form of birth control. This, curiously, is a direct contradiction of another current law, CRS 22-25-104(6)(a) which says sex education, ". . .shall give primary emphasis to abstinence by school-aged children."

The Colorado Department of Human Services is now following through with the new sex ed law. Here is what they said in a publication last year: "...the curricula and training opportunities outlined align with the newly enacted House Bill 19-1032, which requires that sexual health education offered in Colorado be comprehensive, medically accurate, age-appropriate, inclusive of LGBTQ+ populations . . ."[1] HB-1192 takes us to another new term: intersectionality. This is a remake of historical revisionism which will now be imposed on our public-school history curriculums. Intersectionality replaces the major facts and events in a history book with a litany of stories about all potential minority groups that may have been impacted by those events. The recent outcry to destroy historical monuments is one outcome of intersectionality. This law requires history and civics classes to replace the commonly understood history of our nation with this new, progressive agenda.

HB-1120 is an extraordinary reach into parental authority. This bill theoretically gives a 12-year-old child the authority to determine his or her own mental health treatment without parental consent or even notification. I say theoretically because a 12-year-old will not seek mental health treatment on their own. Instead, mental health workers and teachers now become the authority, rather than the parents, for these children as young as 12 years of age. This is a huge violation of the proper jurisdiction of the family.

This brings us to HB-1017. This bill was set up as a pilot program, but the goal of the legislation is to place a mental health worker in every grade in every school. A clear pattern is emerging. Give mental health workers more authority than the parents and make sure they are looking after every child.

HB-1262 dictates to the mental health worker what they can and cannot do. In this case, the new law is banning what is called conversion therapy for minors. This means not allowing any counseling which could help a child confused about their gender to actually choose their biological identity. Instead, they are required to engage in immersion therapy, which reinforces and promotes the child's thought that there is something else out there they should fit into other than their true biological, physical self.

The final bill in the category of education and parental authority is HB-1312, which would have forced all parents to register with the health department for immunization exemptions. After two record-setting public hearings, both having more than 500 people sign up to testify against the bill, the bill passed both House and Senate committees by party-line votes. Then, in the final week of the session, the Democrats killed the bill. In June, after the session was over, Governor Polis issued an executive order implementing as much of HB-1312 as he could without the legislation, and then they got pretty much everything they were looking for in 2020 with SB-163.

The governor and majority party are moving rapidly to replace parents with government control of children.

Global Warming

Driving much of the 2019 major legislation was the anthropogenic carbon dioxide hoax. I am using blunt language to describe this because it is a huge mistake that will destroy much of our state's economy.

Even if increasing levels of carbon dioxide are causing the planet's surface temperatures to significantly increase, of which I find the evidence to be questionable at best, several other factors all need to be absolutely true to justify the radical policies adopted by the 2019 legislature.

First, carbon dioxide must be causing catastrophic changes that outweigh the known catastrophic effects of closing down major parts of our economic production. Second, the increasing levels must be due to human activity. And third, the restrictions on carbon dioxide that Colorado state government is implementing must have a significant, meaningful effect to be justified.

These policies are cloaked in words like health, safety, and clean energy. However, what it really translates into is blackouts, no-drive-days, unemployment, soaring energy costs, economic malaise and a lower standard of living for all of Colorado. If there is any science in this agenda it is political science aimed at amassing greater power for government control at the expense of Colorado's citizens.

Here is a look at the 2019 bills that are now law. In summary, these bills set unrealistic standards for carbon dioxide reduction that will drive up energy costs for production and consumption. They will severely hobble Colorado's economy, reduce government revenues, and make life in Colorado significantly more difficult.

HB-1188 requires all fiscal notes for bills to assess the impact on greenhouse gas emissions, putting this forever before the legislature and the public for all future bills and laying the groundwork for a carbon tax (which some speculate may have been implemented in 2020 with SB-204).

HB-1198 expands a grant program for electric car charging stations. Isn't it ironic that they demand electric utilities lower their carbon dioxide levels, and then give them extra money to increase electricity demand through a state-wide system for charging electric cars?

Which leads us to HB-1261. HB-1261 is, in many ways, the keystone to this agenda. It set up a system to force a reduction in "greenhouse gases" for all of Colorado by 26% by 2025 (less than five years away), 50% by 2030 and 90% by 2050. The Air Quality Control Commission (under the control of the health department) is authorized to implement rules, which are essentially laws, to meet these standards.

HB-1314 put in place a plan to find new lines of work for coal miners. The implication is obvious: they want coal production in Colorado to stop. This means they are intentionally eliminating a major industry in the state and destroying a major Colorado source of power for electric energy.

SB-77 set up a system for charging stations for electric vehicles. This is an intriguing option but, as I mentioned in HB-1198, as they close down coal-fired utilities they also want a fast track to increase electricity use for their new cars.

SB-96 authorized the Health Department to collect data from electric utilities to support the carbon dioxide reductions spelled out in HB-1261.

SB-181 was the big, industry-killing law that put new, heavy regulations on the oil and gas industry. At least 100,000 jobs in Colorado were oil and gas related in 2019. After SB-181 is fully implemented most of that industry, and those high paying jobs, will have left Colorado.

SB-236 reauthorized the Public Utilities Commission. It was initially not a very controversial bill, even though it did originally contain a new cost-factor for carbon emissions. However, in the final week of the session, two other bills, which had previously died, were added to this bill. These last-minute amendments included HB-1313, requiring electric utilities to reduce their carbon dioxide levels 80% by 2030 and 100% by 2050. Also added was HB-1037, authorizing a new fee (higher electric rates) that will help the utilities lower bonding costs for new plant construction, and conveniently increase the profits for utilities.

When I was in the legislature we used to try to encourage a healthy economy, but all these bills that the governor signed in 2019, even without the COVID-19 shutdown, add up to a Polis depression right around the corner.

Red Flag and Criminal Law

It is a bit ironic to group the Red Flag Law, HB-1177, with criminal law. The Red Flag Law is directed by a court and administered by law enforcement, but it is not because anyone has actually broken the law. The Red Flag Law confiscates firearms before the citizen in question breaks any law.

This law requires judges and the police to violate their oaths of office, as it is in conflict with so many provisions of the U.S. and state constitutions (i.e. 2nd, 4th, 5th, 6th, and 14th Amendments). This is why most Colorado counties have said they cannot, and therefore will not, execute the Red Flag Law.

Here is how it works. A law enforcement officer, or someone with a personal connection, a "family or household member," which is very broadly defined, goes to a judge and asks that the gun owner's firearms be taken away. The gun owner is not to be made aware of the hearing for the initial order until after the confiscation order has been issued. Only after the guns have been confiscated (SWAT team at 4:00 AM?) can the owner ask for a hearing to give his or her side of the case. Additionally, the guns cannot be returned to the rightful owner without a background check of that owner.

Remember, this is not because the owner broke any law. It is only based on the concern from someone that a problem may come up in the future. In the Colorado Bill of Rights, Article II, section 13, it states: "the right of no person to keep and bear arms in defense of his home, person and property . . . shall be called in question;" What part of "no person . . . shall be called in question" do they not understand? This is justice turned on its head. But the legislature did not care, and the governor blindly followed and signed it into law.

Another bill, HB-1124 made Colorado a "sanctuary state." Ironically, in the legislative declaration of this bill it says, "Coloradans have constitutional rights to due process and protection against unlawful detainment and seizures." This is the same legislature that passed the Red Flag Law?

HB-1124 makes Colorado a sanctuary state because it prohibits local law enforcement from giving federal immigration authorities information about anyone who committed a crime and is now in jail, or hold that person for pickup by the federal authorities, if it is a civil immigration detainer.

I also find it curious that the "Coloradans" the bill is refers to are illegal aliens, not Colorado citizens. So, it appears that Colorado citizens are not afforded full constitutional protection in the Red Flag Law, but if it is an illegal alien, they will bend over backwards to give them due process and shield the illegal alien from other, justifiable legal processes.

HB-1148 changed certain misdemeanor penalties from one year to 364 days. This sounds rather harmless, but it is another part of the sanctuary state theme. By federal law, a penalty of one year or more triggers a mandatory deportation hearing. Deleting that one day avoids this process, giving illegal aliens who have already been convicted of crimes more opportunities to stay in Colorado.

HB-1266 gives convicted felons on parole the right to vote. The Colorado constitution removes the right to vote while one is serving their "full term of imprisonment" for a felony, which has always included time on parole. This bill weakens that policy by twisting the constitutional phrase "full term of imprisonment" to mean your sentence minus any parole time.

Under this new law, when someone is granted parole, they will automatically be put on the voter registration rolls (SB-235). Being on parole does not mean your sentence is over. It means you are out from behind the prison walls, but still serving the final part of your sentence under the control of the Department of Corrections. Additionally, for many reasons, parole is often revoked, and the person ends back in prison. With HB-1266 and SB-235 the person who was once a parolee, but was then sent back to prison, is now still registered to vote.

Taxes, TABOR and Budgets

Most bills have a financial impact, but for some that is their primary purpose. Here is a brief overview of the most significant financial bills for 2019.

HB-1257 would have eliminated TABOR spending limits if the voters approved the measure at the ballot box. It was called Proposition CC. This was a direct attack on TABOR, the Taxpayer's Bill of Rights. Fortunately the people of Colorado knew more than this legislature and they soundly defeated CC in November of 2019.

HB-1097 would have lowered the state income tax rate to 4.25%. Predictably, it was killed in committee.

HB-1322 authorized the taking of up to $30 million out of the Unclaimed Property Trust Fund every year for three years for an affordable housing program. In 2018, while on the Joint Budget Committee, I sounded the alarm for how much money the state was taking from this trust fund, and now they are set to take another $90 million.

And, as if that was not enough damage to the Unclaimed Property Trust Fund, SB-261 takes another $30 million from the Unclaimed Property Trust Fund. This bill directs the money to the Department of Transportation. I support funding highway construction, but not when we are taking the money from a trust fund of other people's money. If you tried this at home, it would be called grand larceny.

The bottom line is this: The 2019 legislature drove the budget to extreme limits. When all of the obligations from additional programs, like the all-day daycare/kindergarten, the expanded Medicaid system, increasing costs for PERA, and the complete economic meltdown due to the governor's lockdowns in 2020, Colorado cannot continue this spending spree. As the oil and gas industry winds down and increasing energy costs from carbon dioxide reductions kick into high gear we are headed toward an economic brick wall. Socialism never works and we are about to prove it again, here in Colorado.

Laws Affecting Private Businesses

It could easily be argued that all legislation affects business in Colorado because every bill makes the state that much better, or worse — each bill has an impact on the prosperity of our state. However, some bills have a much more direct nexus with the business community and that is what this section concerns.

First, here are three bills that would have been a blessing to the business interests of the state, but they were all quickly killed by this legislature. Not so coincidentally, they all had Republican sponsors. The titles speak for themselves:

HB-1022 Deadly Force Against Intruder at a Business (make-my-day law for businesses)

HB-1097 Income Tax Reduction

SB-053 Ban California Emission Standards for Colorado.

One bad bill was actually killed, HB-1143, prohibiting offering a plastic straw at a restaurant. Straws are now safe, but not Colorado business owners.

Other bills bad for business did become law, including HB-1261, forcing reductions of carbon dioxide. This is the big bill that will severely control industry and individuals in order to meet stringent targets of reducing carbon dioxide; 26% by 2025, 50% by 2030, and 90% by 2050. The power this bill gives to the state health department is breathtaking because they now have the authority to take all of the steps necessary to force these huge reductions of anthropogenic carbon dioxide. Energy costs will skyrocket and at the very least thousands of jobs will be lost forever.

As a companion bill HB-1313 required 80% of carbon dioxide produced by electric utilities to be eliminated by 2030. For this law to be followed, electric utility rates will have to dramatically increase for everyone. This bill was killed, but the language was amended into SB-236, which did pass in the last week of the session and it is now law.

SB-096 collects greenhouse gas emission data. This is part of the plan to make everyone think carbon dioxide is the problem and sets up expectations that more carbon dioxide must be eliminated.

SB-181 increases oil and gas regulations. This is the other big, bad bill, which is now the law of the land. The governor said in his first state of the state address that he was going to shut down oil and gas. SB-181 is the centerpiece of that plan and I cover it in more detail in the next section on property rights.

Property Rights and the 2019 Session

Property owners and their rights were impacted by several pieces of legislation in Colorado in 2019, and none of it was for the good.

The right to own and control private property is an essential part of a free society. Any infringement on this principle erodes our freedoms because free choices in many areas of life are only possible if one can own and control the possessions they need to conduct the affairs of their lives.

I begin with SB-181 Increase Oil and Gas Regulations. This is the biggest taking of private property in the history of the State of Colorado. Everyone in Colorado will feel the effects of this bill as it will increase the cost of energy and the overall economy will be severely challenged. SB-181 is also the end of thousands of jobs in Colorado and many oil and gas related businesses are now going out of business or leaving the state.

This law is an example of how special interests in Denver and Boulder rule over the rest of Colorado. A similar measure was soundly defeated in the 2018 election (Initiative 112). But the anti-energy interests didn't get the message, so they rolled out SB-181 and rolled over the people and rolled over rural Colorado.

All of these are terrible consequences, but the biggest losers are the property owners of oil and gas interests. They cannot move their property. It is just rendered useless by SB-181, losing most or all of its worth. With no regard for the value of these mineral rights, their property interests have been stripped away by new government regulations. For tens of thousands of Colorado citizens, who own millions of acres of mineral rights, the ability to use their oil and gas property has been nearly destroyed by SB-181.

The lost value is incalculable. At a hearing at the Capitol in December of 2019, sponsored by the Republican Study Committee of Colorado, representatives from the Colorado Alliance of Mineral and Royalty Owners testified that the actual value stolen is probably in the trillions of dollars. Their financial expert said that a section (one square mile) of oil producing property can contain $150 million dollars of oil and gas.

The governor is a very rich man. I am certain he would not accept someone coming in and taking all he owns. But he seems to not care much at all when his actions steal vast amounts of property from others.

The Red Flag Law (HB-1177) is another example of a flagrant violation of property rights. In this case it is the firearms of law abiding citizens which can be taken away without due process, without the citizen having broken any law and essentially without their knowledge.

Finally, there are two additional bills I bring to your attention concerning property rights. HB-1322 and SB-261 both take tens of millions of dollars from the Colorado Unclaimed Property Trust Fund. Yes, I said trust fund, which means the state is the fiduciary trustee for unclaimed property of Colorado citizens. If you or I, as a trustee for someone else's money, went ahead and spent it for other purposes we would go to jail. But the legislature and the governor have shown so little regard for the citizens' property rights that they are raiding this fund, again and again. They are raiding it to the extent that the fund may go bankrupt (cannot pay current bills) with another economic downturn in the state. Oh, wait, we are already in the biggest economic downturn in recent history . . .

As I said above, the ability to own and control your property is essential for freedom. In 2019 the governor and his ruling party in the legislature were not defenders of our freedoms. They were rulers, gathering all the power and control for themselves.

Election Laws

As with so many other areas of legislation in 2019, election laws were radicalized. The voting age was lowered with HB-1278, giving 17-year-olds a ballot in primaries if they will turn 18 on or before the general election. This effectively moves the voting age down by about six months in presidential election years.

HB-1243, which did not make it into law, would have given 16-year-olds a ballot in all school-related questions, including bond elections and school board elections.

HB-1278 did make into law and it mandated big changes in the number of voting centers and ballot drop boxes, and it requires vote centers on college campuses. At one point every county clerk in the state opposed this bill.

Early in the session, SB-042, the National Popular Vote for Presidential Elections, (NPV) was passed and signed by the governor. The NPV will radically overturn the system we have for electing the president and it has the potential of doing much damage to our civil government.

It severely upsets the balance of power between the states and the federal government and it will deny all states not in the compact any meaningful role in selecting the president.

The NPV violates several parts of the Constitution: Article I, Section 10, Article II, Section 1, Article V, and the Twelfth Amendment. If it is implemented, it may lead to a significant constitutional crisis.

In the current system, the states elect the president, but with the NPV individual state authority and influence will be severely diminished. Consequently, the NPV will concentrate more power into the federal government and the people on the east and west coasts will elect the President.

The proponents argue that in Article I each state is given the authority to determine how their electors are selected, and all the NPV does is direct that state to ignore the will of their own citizens and follow the national vote totals. However, they are using this clause to completely destroy the reason the Electoral College system was created, which is to empower the states to elect the President.

The NPV is designed to become effective if a bare minimum of 270 electoral votes are controlled by the states participating in the compact. This would force at least 20-30 additional states, who never adopted the compact, to live under this new rule.

The wording within the NPV bill does not require the approval of Congress, even though Congressional approval is a constitutional mandate for all state compacts that affect the balance of powers between the states and the federal government.

Additionally, the NPV directly violates a little-known part of the Colorado Constitution. At the very end of the Colorado Constitution there is a "Schedule," which gives final implementing instructions for the General Assembly. In Section 20 it requires the General Assembly to provide a system after 1876 (the first year of Colorado statehood) where the electors to the Electoral College are chosen by a direct vote of the people. The NPV will strip this away from the voters of Colorado.

That's the bad news. Here is the good news. For the first time in many decades, an initiative was successful in challenging a bill passed by the General Assembly, and the National Popular Vote bill will be reviewed by the people by vote in the November 2020 election.

As mentioned in a previous section of this chapter, a constitutionally-established part of the penalty for felony crimes in Colorado is that you cannot vote until you have finished your prison sentence, which includes time spent on parole. HB-1266 gave all parolees the right to vote. This is a violation of the Colorado constitution, but the legislature and the governor didn't care and in 2019 made HB-1266 law.

Finally, SB-235, Automatic Voter Registration, may be the worst of all the new election laws here in Colorado, ever. It directs all state agencies to register to vote everyone who contacts their office for any reason. This includes Medicaid, where at least 25% of the population is on their roles. SB-235 will result in the state automatically registering many thousands of non-citizens. Election integrity was significantly compromised by SB-235.

Summary

As the conclusion of my observations of Colorado's 2019 legislative session here is the impact these new laws will have on Colorado's culture, values, and future.

Public Schools

A clear agenda was mapped out for the nearly 900,000 public school students with the intersex bill, also known as the sex ed bill, HB-1032, the intersectionality bill, HB-1192, the 12-year-old mental health bill, HB-1120, the immersion therapy bill, HB-1262, the put a mental health worker in every grade of every school bill, HB-1017, and the force all parents to register with the health department for immunization exemptions, HB-1312. This was the immunization bill which was killed at the end of the 2019 session, but then the governor issued an executive order implementing as much of the bill as he could without the actual legislation, and in 2020 SB-163 implemented the agenda of HB-1312.

Not directly affecting public schools, but along the same value structure as this crop of bills, was HB-1039 requiring birth certificates, drivers' licenses and other identity documents to list several options for gender, with the applicant choosing any of the options: male, female, X, or ?

When all of these bills are seen together, there is a clear pattern of normalizing the abnormal, removing parents' authority, dictating the therapy options for licensed mental health professionals, and putting the schools at the center of this new values paradigm. Public schools are becoming less of a place for education and more of a place for indoctrination.

Of course COVID-19 and the governor's excessive edicts have now thrown a monkey wrench into the public school system, so it may be that they over played their hand and the public school monopoly will be replaced by a more reasonable balance of parental control through public, private and homeschooling in Colorado.

Immigration

The most significant bill in this area is HB-1124, which makes Colorado a sanctuary state. The bill prohibits a law enforcement officer from arresting or detaining an individual solely on the basis of a civil immigration detainer from the U.S. Immigration and Customs Enforcement Agency, and it prohibits a probation officer or probation department employee from providing an individual's personal information to federal immigration authorities.

Both of these bills reflect a new policy in Colorado of turning a blind eye to any immigration violations.

RSCC trip to Texas/Mexico Border
Representative Saine (left), Texas National Guard guide (middle), Senator Sonnenberg (right)

Criminal Law

Most egregious in this category is the Red Flag Law, HB-1177 because it treats law-abiding citizens like criminals and does not even give them the due process afforded to real criminals. This law now pits average citizens against local police, significantly eroding trust in our law enforcement officers. It also sets up a path for greater gun confiscation. With all of the undeserved animus currently being directed at the police, HB-1177 is making it that much harder for them to properly do their job.

HB-1266 defies the state constitution by giving felons voting privileges before they complete their sentences (while on parole). This is another way of twisting our voting system and eroding the penalty system for felonies.

Elections

Speaking of elections, the overall attitude of the 2019 session was to abandon any pretense of voter integrity, as seen in HB-1266 (discussed above), HB-1278 (wholesale changes in election policies, including 17½-year-olds voting in primaries), SB-235 (automatic voter registration) and SB-42, the National Popular Vote law.

These new election laws make voter fraud more probable and reduce our confidence in the integrity of the election system in Colorado.

Private Property Rights

A cornerstone of our freedoms is property rights, for no one is truly free unless they can own and control their private property. Many bills in 2019 showed little regard for the citizen's right to control their own property. Renters bills (HB-1106, HB-1118, and HB-1170), government raids on the Unclaimed Property Trust Fund (HB-1322 and SB-261) and destroying uncounted trillions of dollars in mineral property assets with the oil and gas regulations (SB-181), all show a clear pattern of not valuing or honoring the unalienable rights of property owners.

Global Warming

Finally, of all the bills driving the state toward a fool's errand, it is the global warming bills that are key. With these new laws, we are abandoning the energy sector in our state and dooming the people to rationing and sky-high energy costs; all this to follow a manufactured value of thinking that the biggest threat to mankind is the sort of stuff that comes out of your mouth with every breath, carbon dioxide. It is economic, cultural and scientific madness that drives this newfound value, which the governor and legislature have wholly embraced.

The bills in this list are: HB-1261, HB-1313, HB-1314, SB-96, and SB-236.

The global warming frenzy captured the 2019 legislature and we will all pay dearly for their insanity. As the state's economy continues to slide downhill it is much more than the COVID-19 pandemic. You can thank the governor and the legislature for much of this calamity.

It is not overstating the situation to say the radical new values being forced on the people of Colorado are driving our state backward. I hope and pray that it is not too late to turn this around and get back on a track of wholesome values that promote prosperity, integrity and freedom for the citizens of Colorado.

NOTES

1. CO4Kids.org *Colorado Sexual Health Initiative (CoSHI) is now a part of Office of Children, Youth and Families (OCYF).* July 2, 2019. https://co4kids.org/community/colorado-sexual-health-initiative-coshi-now-part-ocyf

2

A PANDEMIC OF HUBRIS: COMPUTER MODELS TURN "EVIDENCE-BASED GUESSWORK' INTO GOSPEL

BY KARL DIERENBACH
Engineer and Attorney

The response to the coronavirus in Colorado is a tale of faith and devotion. Not toward the people of Colorado or God, but to a handful of academics and a model they created. It is a tale of hubris in that the model, and the assumptions baked into it, became sacrosanct. As such, the predictive outputs of the model drove Colorado's responses, unchallenged by anyone or anything. Conflicting opinions and actions were literally considered deadly and conflicting data was simply ignored. As a result, businesses were shuttered, 340,000[1] Coloradans lost their jobs and immeasurable pain was inflicted, largely to avoid the model's fantastic doomsday scenarios.

The model was infallible in that it was designed such that any outcome would fall within its range of predictions and any model-generated value, such as a measure of social distancing, would be used as the sole measure of Coloradans' obedience to orders. So, for example, if hospitalizations climbed, the model would say it's because social distancing dropped to some value, such as for example, 45%. The 45% wouldn't be derived from a study of behavior, it was simply what the model said must have happened to produce the hospitalization increase. The model's self-validation limited criticism (how do you argue against 45%?) and enabled it to carry more and more influence over policy.

Early Panic

The model was born in panic and developed in desperation. Images of makeshift Wuhan hospitals, the news of the first COVID-19 death in the U.S., and the announcement of Colorado's first case on March 5, 2020, set the backdrop for Colorado Governor Jared Polis' declaration of a state of emergency on March 11. Three days later, Colorado saw its first COVID-19 death and Polis held a press conference to discuss Colorado's strategy. Standing before an easel supporting a "Flatten the Curve" poster, Polis explained[2] that a goal of Colorado's response was to slow the spread of COVID-19 such that Colorado's hospitals would not be overwhelmed, which would lead to rationing care as was being experienced in Italy.

It is important to note that the idea behind flattening the curve was not to avoid significant numbers of hospitalizations, but to spread out their occurrence such that no one is denied access to healthcare due to lack of available resources. Likewise, deaths are not *avoided* by flattening the curve, they are only *delayed*. Polis basically acknowledged this when he lamented, "Under some projections most

Americans will likely get coronavirus."

Meanwhile, a paper[3] released on March 16 from Imperial College London gained worldwide attention for its prediction of 2.2 million deaths in the United States if we did nothing in response to the coronavirus. Colorado's share of such a disaster would be about 39,000 fatalities. For reference, Colorado's portion of the 2017-2018 flu season's 61,000 U.S. deaths was likely around 1,000.

Also on March 16, the Governor's Expert Emergency Epidemic Response Committee (GEEERC) held a meeting where they discussed Colorado's response to the coronavirus. The committee discussed possible responses and as a first step recommended the closing of bars, restaurants, gyms, theaters and casinos in Colorado. A few hours after the meeting, Polis did just that.[4] Two days later, Polis would close schools and ban gatherings of more than 10 people. GEEERC also discussed additional closures that would be implemented in the following days. The committee was not working with a lot of information, with one member declaring, "What we're embarking on here is evidence-informed guesswork."

Modeling

It was during this early period that the COVID-19 Modeling Group (CMG) was formed and began preparing estimates of infections, hospitalizations and deaths due to COVID-19 and feeding that information to the Polis administration. The group was staffed[5] with professors and post doctorate fellows with one person from the Colorado Department of Public Health and Environment (CDPHE) who had earned a PhD in 2019. Over the next several months the CMG would produce multiple reports on the estimated damage caused by COVID-19 in terms of hospitalizations and fatalities. What the group lacked was any sense of the collateral damage their recommendations would do to society.

In a March 27 press conference,[6] Governor Polis discussed the CMG's first publically released report and its prediction of 33,200 deaths by June 1, 2020 if Coloradans did not immediately begin social distancing. This was a horrifying prediction, particularly when considering that, at the time, Colorado had suffered only 31 deaths from COVID-19. However, the number did align well with the Imperial College London prediction for the US.

March 27 Press Conference

What was just as concerning as the numbers being presented was how they were being presented. Aside from the occasional lip service to the model being an estimation of the real world, the model was generally treated as gospel by all government officials and the media. This was troubling since the model's main input used to project future trends was the percentage of social distancing practiced by Coloradans and that value was derived from the model itself. This was done by basing Coloradans social distancing performance on hospitalizations that occurred a few days later.

This aspect was explicitly described, for example, in CMG's July 16 report[7] in which they stated, "We note that due to the approximately 13-day lag between infection and hospitalization, we are currently able to estimate social distancing through late June." In other words, once they see how many people are hospitalized, they can tell you what must have been the social distancing level of 13 days ago. This isn't necessarily a bad feature of a model. Indeed, to make models as accurate as possible, it is reasonable to continually update them with the latest information.

However, such results should at least be put to the smell test. For example, on May 29, the CMG reported[8] that during the Stay at Home order Coloradans socially distanced at a rate of 80% (0% would be no social distancing and 100% would be no contact whatsoever). Then when the Stay at Home order was lifted for much of Colorado, the model suggested Coloradans increased their social distancing to 85%. It seems unlikely that Coloradans, in a time where hospitalizations were plummeting and restrictions were easing, would actually increase their reclusiveness. Yet the data goes unchallenged because the model is deemed infallible.

It is this reverence for the model and the underlying assumptions used in creating it that did the most damage to Colorado. As noted, the originally released model data showed Colorado suffering 33,200 deaths by June 1 and this number aligned well with the Imperial College London study. However, where the Imperial College London study was subsequently panned for being poorly crafted and wildly overly pessimistic, subsequent CMG predictions went the other way. In their April 6 report,[9] the CMG, inexplicably and without explanation, changed their June 1 "0% social distancing efficacy" prediction to 73,162 deaths with total deaths of over 80,000 by January 1, 2021! This value was criticized and after the April 6 report, subsequent reports no longer predicted fatalities, although the underlying assumptions remained basically unchanged.

The 80,000 potential fatalities was wildly out of step with other epidemiologists and with real-life results and evidence from around the world. 80,000 Deaths in Colorado's population of 5.8 million is a population mortality rate of 1.4%. To put that in perspective, if the entire world saw that mortality level, COVID-19 would kill 109 million people. In the U.S., that rate would translate into over 4.5 million deaths. Nobody but the CMG was predicting such causalities. At the 1.4% population mortality rate, Sweden, where they never went into lockdown and never closed primary schools, would suffer 140,000 deaths. As of July 30, 2020, Sweden[10] had experienced 5,739 COVID-19 fatalities and was seeing around 1 new COVID-19 death a day. None of this seemed to be on the radar of the CMG.

While the world was taking in new information and updating predictions, the CMG was doggedly sticking to their March predictions[11] and not allowing any outside information to alter their path. On March 30, Polis noted that Colorado needed 9 or 10 thousand ventilators.[12] Colorado hit its peak ventilator usage of 471 on April 16.[13] Colorado spent tens of millions of dollars[14] to have the Army Corps of Engineers convert the Colorado Convention Center into a makeshift hospital that never saw a single patient. Yet, none of these misfires caused the CMG to rethink their assumptions.

Despite predicted mortality rates out of step with the rest of the world, real-world data indicating their fatality estimates are too high, and wildly over estimating resource requirements, the CMG basically stuck to their guns regarding the lethality of COVID-19 from March through the end of July (at the time of this writing).

Fundamentally, the CMG's model has four key control measures:[15] social distancing, mask wearing, identification and isolation of cases, and contact tracing. Everything else seems to have remained basically unchanged from March through the end of July. That is, the underlying assumptions of infection fatality rates, basic (unmitigated) reproduction number, and asymptomatic rates seem to be unwavering. Furthermore, the model does not seem to contemplate any percentage of society having an innate or preexisting resistance to infection.

And therein lays the root problem of the CMG's self-validating model: massive death if we do nothing, and the only significant variable used is social distancing.

(Mis)Using the Model to Guide Policy

To understand how the model became gospel to Gov. Polis and controlled his response, you must understand Polis. He has a tendency to latch onto a study or claim that supports his world view and follow it while disregarding any evidence to the contrary. For example, he based claims[16] that state provided pre-school is a good investment based on tiny studies that claimed kids who attend pre-school are less likely to serve prison sentences later in life. Yet Polis completely disregards large Head Start studies[17] that show the effects of preschool dissipate during elementary school. In other words, Polis selects experts that support his agenda and world view and ignores other sources. This appears to be happening with respect to COVID-19.

The threat from the coronavirus put Polis in a position to declare a state of emergency and take on tremendous power. On March 25, Governor Polis issued a state-wide Stay at Home order scheduled to last through April 11. Given the magnitude of the number of predicted deaths from the model, the escalating number of hospitalizations and the expected limited duration of the order, there seemed to be little consideration of conflicting values and identifiable trade-offs. Indeed, in confronting the COVID-19 threat, Governor Polis appeared to give the recommendations of the CMG experts and their models an unprecedented monopoly over predicting the future.

Governor Polis would maintain his state of emergency through the summer of 2020, never seriously considering the trade-offs involved – a far cry from the deliberative policy process one would hope our government would undertake when enacting such widespread and oppressive orders.

As noted, in early April the CMG upped the ante by reporting that the lockdowns were preventing 80,000 deaths. Thus all of Polis' decisions were supported by the belief his actions were the demarcation between life and death for tens of thousands. Under these conditions, over time the model outputs became sacrosanct, for they were the source of his power and the justifications for his actions. If the models were wrong, that would mean Polis' actions were wrong. You can see this progression in Polis' press briefings. Early in the pandemic, the model was sometimes described with a degree of humility. As time went by, the model's outputs were treated more and more like iron-clad representations of the real world.

This combination of infallible quasi-scientific models and the government's responsibility for staving off massive fatalities had tremendous negative effects. Foremost is that there may have been up to one non- COVID-19 death caused by the lockdown[18] for every two to four COVID-19 deaths. During the height of the Stay at Home orders, emergency rooms across the country saw massive declines in patients. ER doctors, for example, reported seeing less heart attack and stroke victims and the ones they were seeing were more serious than normal. People who would have normally gone to a doctor or ER due to trauma were delaying or skipping the trip in fear of catching COVID-19. Many healthcare professionals were actively telling people to stay away from doctors and ERs if at all possible. In the U.S., these delays likely caused tens of thousands of non- COVID-19 fatalities. Moreover, missed or delayed treatments for cancer and other ailments and reduction of screenings may have negative ramifications for years to come.

The massive number of predicted deaths justified reactions that were catastrophic:

- destroyed 340,000 jobs in Colorado,
- contributed greatly to the intensity of social unrest after the horrific death of George Floyd,
- destroyed countless businesses both large and small,
- likely caused numerous deaths of despair due to suicide and substance abuse,
- likely enabled significant increases in domestic abuse and child abuse,
- delayed the education of over a million of Colorado's children,

- delayed elective surgeries and medical treatment for thousands of people,
- created a huge budget shortfall diminishing public services and benefits,
- diminished the quality of life of millions of Coloradans.

None of the above "side effects" worked their way into the CMG's modeling.

The sheer number Polis and the CMG believed would die if Colorado returned to normal also led to a fundamental change in Colorado's response: they completely abandoned "Flatten the Curve" and moved to "Hunker Down until a Vaccine." This was made explicit in Governor Polis' June 15 press conference[19] where he described the "Protect Our Neighbors" phase of Colorado's COVID-19 response as, "the phase that is the way we have to live until there is a vaccine or cure."

In truth, they were trying to win an unwinnable battle.

Dr. Rachel Herlihy, whom Polis called the state's top epidemiologist, has said[20] that we "must continue to be vigilant if we are going to defeat this virus." Flatten the curve said that you can't defeat coronavirus, you can only delay it to prevent healthcare system overload. But now Colorado's top epidemiologist was declaring the goal of defeating coronavirus when over 50,000 Coloradans had tested positive for the virus. By the end of July, Polis was speaking[21] of the effort to "crush this virus" and all semblance of rationality was gone.

Few commentators or news reports have pointed out the obvious: *No one voted for this, not even the state's elected legislators.* Only one Coloradan made the decision to hunker down until a vaccine is available – Governor Polis. He made the decision and Colorado was thrown into perpetual semi-lockdown with a government official exercising perpetual emergency powers — justified by the 80,000 deaths he was allegedly preventing.

When you are preventing 80,000 deaths, almost anything can be justified, such as Stay at Home orders where, for the first time in our state's history, healthy people are told they can't leave their homes under threat[22] of fines and imprisonment for up to one year.

The threat of 80,000 deaths can justify basically calling people (and neighbors and coworkers) "murderers" just because they want to eat at a restaurant on Mother's Day. In response to such an illegal celebration of motherhood, Polis claimed[23] the lack of adherence to his social distancing orders can make the difference "between going on living or suffering a particularly agonizing, painful and lonely death." This is absurd since Polis' own claimed policy is meant to suppress the virus to a manageable level, which implies allowing a certain number of people to die from COVID-19. Again, it is Polis' hubris that allows him and him alone to determine what risk level Colorado should maintain. *His* determination of acceptable levels of death is noble, while the people's is selfish and murderous.

Since Polis and the CMG believe there is an almost unlimited number of fatalities that will befall Coloradans if they open up too much, they have created an atmosphere of constant fear that the next surge is right around the corner. Instead of fostering resolution to weather a storm, they placed the blame for any surge on a disobedient population — typically Republicans and conservatives who value individualism above collectivism.

Treating Colorado citizens like impetuous teenagers, Polis frequently warned them that if they didn't change their behavior, punishment would follow. Regarding lockdowns, in early April Polis warned,[24] "If there is any way to safely end it sooner, then we will. And likewise, if Coloradans aren't staying at home and the numbers of the dead and dying continue to increase, then it could go longer." In late April, he proudly displayed a graphic[25] at a news conference that read, "LET ME BE CLEAR: IF PEOPLE DON'T DO THEIR PART — We will go back to Stay at Home."

This tactic creates a no-lose political dynamic for Polis. If hospitalizations and deaths go down, he will claim it was his leadership that saved the day. If they go up, Polis will simply blame the people for not doing what they were told. And here's the most insidious part: the model will back him up either way. Since the model is simply a formula that takes hospitalizations experienced as an input and spits out a social distancing level as an output, any rise in hospitalizations will be attributed to a theoretical fall in social distancing levels. So, if hospitalizations go up, the model will say it must be because social distancing dipped; then Colorado's czar will blame the people and institute another restriction.

Many of Colorado's coronavirus response shortcomings were displayed in late June and July when, after two months of decreasing hospitalizations, the pace of reduction slowed and then hospitalizations began to increase. At the time, COVID-19 hospitalizations occupied a little over 1% of Colorado's hospital beds. Colorado's healthcare system was not under any threat of being overwhelmed; yet the CMG sprang into action and produced a new, official projection predicting the path of hospitalizations (below).[26]

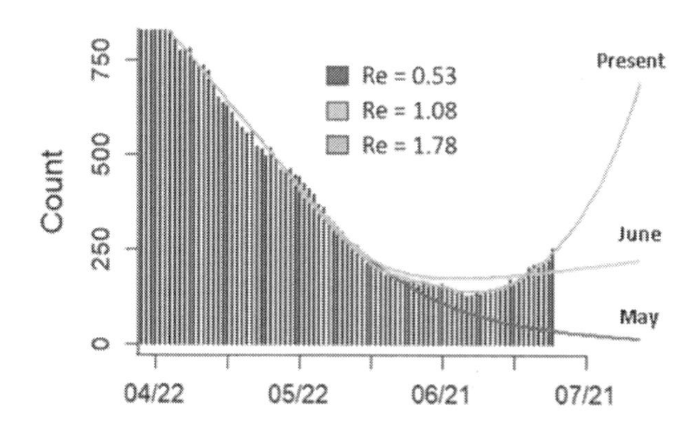

Figure 3. The projected trajectory of COVID-19 hospitalizations if Colorado social distancing levels remained at levels seen in May after the full state transition to Safer at home (5/9-5/26, 89% red line), in June (5/27-7/1, 66% blue line), or at present estimated levels (6/21-7/1, 41% yellow line).

True to form, the health department's graph showed a frightening scenario of an uncontrolled surge in hospitalizations. Also true to form, the prediction turned out to be a massive overestimation and almost immediately the rise slowed and hospitalizations began to fall again.[27]

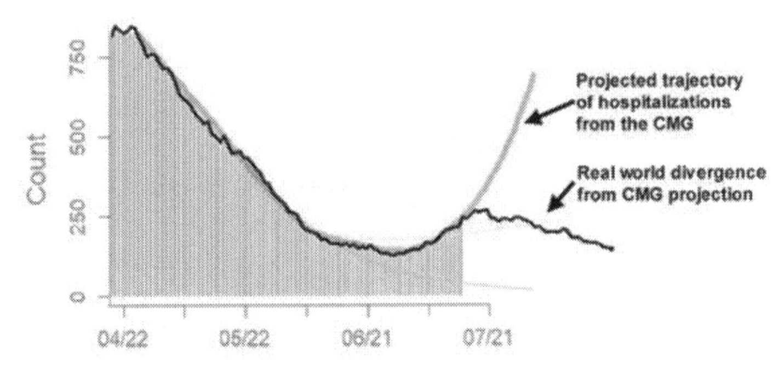

Graph of the COVID-19 Modeling Group projected trajectory of hospitalizations (from previous graph) overlayed with the actual number of people hospitalized with COVID-19 from the CDPHE showing real world divergence from the CMG projection.

Also true to form, Polis took the opportunity to issue more mandates, including the reclosing of bars and mandating that all Coloradans over ten years of age wear masks when in indoor public places. Originally, flatten the curve was about avoiding overwhelming hospitals, but by mid-July, a slight uptick from COVID-19 patients occupying 1% of Colorado's hospital beds drove Polis to increase restrictions. All perspective was lost.

With respect to masks, they went from not even being mentioned as a mitigation tool in early April to being absolutely essential in July. Indeed, Polis has declared[28], "The modeling shows that if we want to avoid a catastrophic breach of our health care system, and if we want to re-open our economy to a greater degree, then masks are absolutely essential." Yet the CMGs modeling shows masks have a tiny effect in relation to the effect of social distancing. It is hard to see masks being essential when the entire modeled effect of mandating them can be hidden within the noise associated with social distancing. This could lead one to suspect that masks have become more of a political issue than a public health issue.

Finally with respect to masks, in true Polis fashion, he attempted[29] to sell the masks as good for the economy, citing a study that declared that wearing masks was worth trillions of dollars to the economy, despite the fact that wearing a mask is a constant reminder that disease is just outside of your lips, and but for a piece of cloth, you are dead. A mask is worn out of fear, and fear generally is not economically stimulative.

Another effect of the thinking that there were tens of thousands of potential deaths if the state opened up is COVID-19 cases became elevated in importance to an irrational level. Remember, flatten the curve was all about keeping hospitals from being overwhelmed. Accordingly, hospitals should have been the driving force in policy. However, under the idea that increases in the number of cases leads to proportional increases in the number of hospitalizations, Polis looked to cases to inform decisions.

However, as the pandemic wore on, the relation between cases and hospitalizations changed. One reason for the phenomenon was that as testing capacity increased beyond the level needed for those with serious symptoms, more and more people with mild or no symptoms were able to be tested. Since Colorado was now detecting more cases that were not in need of hospitalizations, the percentage of positive results needing hospitalizations plummeted. Also, as society opened up, many more relatively young people were catching COVID-19, who also rarely needed hospitalization.

These twin factors of testing healthier people and more

younger people catching COVID-19 meant that the relationship between cases and hospitalizations had shifted radically around May and June. Below is a graph of Colorado Department of Public Health and Environment (CDPHE) case and hospital data. The number of cases found March through May coincided with hospitalized numbers in excess of 800 hospitalizations. However, a similar number of cases detected in July and August accompanied about a quarter of the cases seen in March through May.

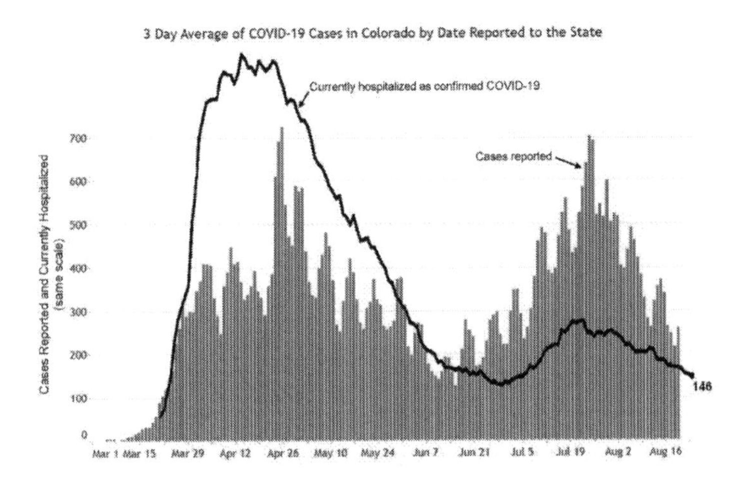

3 Day Average of COVID-19 Cases in Colorado by Date Reported to the State

However, this did not stop Polis and the CDPHE from using cases throughout the epidemic as a driver of policy even though after May Colorado's hospital capacity wasn't threatened. Throughout the COVID-19 mess, Polis and the CDPHE used a system where any two cases in a facility or non-household group constituted an outbreak. Such a low threshold enabled Polis to rely on a continuous stream of outbreaks to maintain public anxiety. As of August 20, 2020 the number of outbreaks listed by CDPHE was 561. Calling two or more cases an "outbreak" also had the effect of frightening Coloradans and pushing them toward more radical reactions in response. Instead of a calming force, Polis and the CDPHE provided a constant stream of alarmism.

For example in August, Fort Lupton High School closed the entire school for two weeks when two students were tested positive for COVID-19. This while the number of hospital beds in Colorado with COVID-19 patients was less than 2% of Colorado's capacity and Colorado was seeing two to five COVID-19 deaths per day. Moreover, it was an "outbreak" among high school students for whom catching COVID-19 is less lethal than catching the flu; far less lethal. The risk to high school students of dying from COVID-19 is minuscule, and for teachers under 65, the risk of death is comparable to or less than the risk from catching the flu.

Speaking of schools, despite a continuous stream of hopeful contemplations such as the Trump Administration's "15 Days to Slow the Spread" and Governor Polis' own plans for reopening, when President Trump began to talk in July about reopening schools, Jon Samet, the head of the CMG, immediately accused Trump of political motivations. Samet basically accused Trump of using the opening of schools to bolster his reelection chances, writing,[30] "The Trump Administration and others have intertwined school reopening with politics, and the symbolism of a return to signaling 'normalcy' in the fall at the time of the November election (enough said)." This was in a letter where Samet himself discussed the benefits of returning to school, and in the same month that the CDC was announcing that the benefits to children of returning to school outweighed any risks. But if Trump says that, well it couldn't be because he wants kids to go back to school and families to have a more normal life.

Summary

The story of Colorado's handling of the coronavirus is one of hubris: hubris on the part of Polis acting as protector of Colorado and treating its citizens like reckless children who must be ordered around for their own good; and hubris on the part of the COVID-19 Modeling Group who assumed coronavirus lethality to be far greater than most experts and never wavered from that belief despite contradictory evidence from Colorado and around the world.

The CMG created an un-falsifiable model that essentially counted hospitalizations and spat out a social distancing value. The value was then treated as inviolable – even if it made no sense. And if the real-world outcomes were not satisfactory, the model's "scientifically" derived threat of massive fatalities was used to justify emergency orders and/or to terrify and intimidate Coloradans into obedience.

Governor Polis, who is always ready to extol experts who support his world view, went all in and treated the model as gospel. No countervailing information was allowed into his realm. Armed with the righteousness of ostensibly saving tens of thousands of lives, Polis seized power and unilaterally suspended, changed and created laws by Executive Order as he saw fit. The fact that his actions led to hundreds of thousands of Coloradans losing their jobs, a million children booted from schools, and immeasurable suffering foisted on Coloradans, was all justified and sustained by the exaggerated predictions of his anointed soothsayers. His orders were to be obeyed under threat of being ordered to stay at home or of having livelihoods destroyed. Put simply, if Coloradans did not do as King Polis demanded, he would take away their stuff and put them in time-out.

NOTES

1. Svaldi, Aldo. The Denver Post. *Colorado regains a fifth of jobs lost during pandemic in May*. June 19, 2020
https://www.denverpost.com/2020/06/19/colorado-jobs-may-covid/

2. Update on COVID-19 in Colorado. Video – Facebook, March 13, 2020
https://www.facebook.com/watch/live/?v=619707838607508&ref=watch_permalink

3. Imperial College London COVID-19 Response Team, *Report 9: Impact of non-pharmaceutical interventions (NPIs) to reduce COVIID-19 mortality and healthcare demands.* March 16, 2020
https://www.imperial.ac.uk/media/imperial-college/medicine/sph/ide/gida-fellowships/Imperial-College-COVID19-NPI-modelling-16-03-2020.pdf

4. Ingold, John. The Colorado Sun. *A special committee advises the governor on how to respond to an epidemic. They're never face a test like this.* March 17, 2020
https://coloradosun.com/2020/03/17/polis-epidemic-response-coronavirus-cdphe/

5. The COVID-19 Epidemic Curve for Colorado and Denver. April 1, 2020
https://drive.google.com/file/d/1VqLN9Qjd6v8Xb9f7LfCalb29NF572pL6/view

6. Update on COVID-19 in Colorado. Video – Facebook, March 27, 2020
https://www.facebook.com/jaredpolis/videos/218356769522217

7. Colorado COVID-19 Modeling Group. *The current state of COVID-19 in Colorado and projected course of the epidemic in the coming weeks.* July 16, 2020.
https://www.ucdenver.edu/docs/librariesprovider151/default-document-library/modeling-report-2020-07-16.pdf?sfvrsn=3922c2b9_2

8. Colorado COVID-19 Modeling Group. *The current state of COVID-19 in Colorado and projected course of the epidemic in the coming weeks.* May 29, 2020.

https://drive.google.com/file/d/1ZCX_mloh0kQS-c9-UdPjqlBRVAovQnJl/view

9. *Projections of the COVID-19 epidemic in Colorado under different social distancing scenarios* April 6, 2020 https://wp-cpr.s3.amazonaws.com/uploads/2020/04/COVIDModelingReport_2020.04.06.pdf

10. Worldometer. Coronavirus Cases – Sweden https://www.worldometers.info/coronavirus/country/sweden/

11. Interview Jonathan Samet, Dean of the Colorado School of Public Health (KUNC TV), July 30, 2020 https://www.facebook.com/KUNC915/videos/932045697307045

12 . Update on COVID-19 in Colorado by Governor Polis. Video – Facebook, March 30, 2020 https://www.facebook.com/jaredpolis/videos/201921554576381

13. Colorado Department of Public Health and Environment. *Colorado COVID-19 hospital data.* Updated Aug. 17, 2020. https://covid19.colorado.gov/hospital-data

14. Sylte, Allison. 9News. *Empty Colorado Convention Center field hospital wants more money.* June 24, 2020. https://www.9news.com/article/news/local/next/empty-colorado-convention-center-field-hospital/73-f872dd65-e52b-4951-bf1d-02063ec156d7

15. Colorado COVID-19 Modeling Group Colorado *COVID-19 Mathematical Model Documentation,* July 1, 2020 https://cucovid19.shinyapps.io/colorado/_w_1dc0c5c2/SEIR%20Documentation_29290701.pdf

16. TEDxBoulder – Jared Polis – *Financing Mechanism for Developing Human Capital.* YouTube, Dec 23, 2010 https://www.youtube.com/watch?v=1kXEbQXzvxE

17. *Head Start Research: Third Grade Follow-up to the Head Start Impact Study – Final Report OPRE Report 2012-45.* October 2012. https://www.acf.hhs.gov/sites/default/files/opre/head_start_report.pdf

18. Dierenbach, Karl. *Dierenbach: The coronavirus response has been deadly.* July 11, 2020.
https://pagetwo.completecolorado.com/2020/06/11/dierenbach-the-coronavirus-response-has-been-deadly/

19. Gov. Polis provides update on COVID-19 in Colorado. June 15, 2020
https://www.facebook.com/jaredpolis/videos/2751089851881550

20. Weekly update by Governor Jared Polis June 30
https://www.facebook.com/jaredpolis/videos/192986595469829

21. Governor Polis provides update on State's response to COVID-19 July 30, 2020. Posted at Colorado.gov
https://www.colorado.gov/governor/news/governor-polis-provides-update-states-response-covid-19-1

22. *Amended Public Health Order 20-24 Implementing Stay at Home Requirements,* March 25, 2020. Colorado Department of Public Health & Environment
https://drive.google.com/file/d/1IzfYUaxEf-UFSVAzkY_b9Cf1OMPOdlxH/view

23. Puckett, Nick. Castle Rock News-Press. *State suspending Castle Rock restaurant's business license after it defies public health order.* May 11, 2020
https://castlerocknewspress.net/stories/colorado-suspending-c-and-c-castle-rock-restaurant-license,298858

24. Burness, Alex. Denver Post. *Colorado Gov. Jared Polis extends statewide stay-at-home order to April 26.*
https://www.denverpost.com/2020/04/06/coronavirus-colorado-jared-polis-address-covid/

25. #DoingMyPartCO Presentation, March 27, 2020
https://drive.google.com/file/d/1KGgq_8NiuzCmo5TT6rFhssPF4Aqe_Pl7/view

26. Colorado COVID-19 Modeling Group Report Chart – Figure 3 – July 16, 2020
https://www.ucdenver.edu/docs/librariesprovider151/default-document-library/modeling-report-2020-07-16.pdf?sfvrsn=3922c2b9_2

27. Chart showing Divergence from prediction

https://covid19.colorado.gov/data

28. *Governor Polis Launches Campaign Encouraging Coloradans to Wear Masks, Provides Update on COVID-19 Response.* June 4, 2020 https://www.colorado.gov/governor/news/governor-polis-launches-campaign-encouraging-coloradans-wear-masks-provides-update-covid-19

29. Latest on COIV-19 in Colorado July 9, 2020 https://www.facebook.com/jaredpolis/videos/395716821388695

30. Samet, Jonathan. Colorado School of Public Health. *Dean's COVID-19 Commentary.* July 27, 2020 https://coloradosph.cuanschutz.edu/resources/covid-19/deans-covid-19-commentary/public-health-main-site-news/covid-19-back-to-school

3

GOVERNMENT BY EXECUTIVE DECREE: COLORADO IN UNCHARTED WATERS

BY KELLY SLOAN
Public Affairs Consultant

The COVID-19 pandemic — and more specifically, the government's various reactions to it — tested many of the most basic concepts of Western liberal democracy — including the rule of law, separation of powers, the principle of subsidiary, and the very role of government – in ways few previous peacetime crises have done. Unhappily, few of the venerable institutions of civil life that Americans have come to take for granted have emerged unscathed.

The system that Americans first inherited from the British (which was itself honed over centuries dating back to Greek and Roman antiquity) and then forged into the "more perfect" constitutional republic that was vouchsafed us, was intended by the framers to hold up even – perhaps especially – in the most trying and unusual of times. Nevertheless, in many cases in Colorado during the turbulent months of 2020, those pillars of governance appeared to be regarded as little more than an anachronistic curiosity, readily disposable as expediency demanded.

To be sure, there have been several instances in America's past where either existential necessity or more basal political ambition have resulted in strains or outright abuses of the constitutional system and the Bill of Rights. For instance, few would succeed in defending the Alien and Sedition Act as being consistent with the principles of the founding documents signed only a few short years prior. President Lincoln's suspension of *Habeas Corpus* during the Civil War has received from historians both praise for its wartime pragmatism and approbation from those who viewed it as an abuse of power.

Much has been written on the political excesses and constitutional circumlocutions of FDR; and, of course, over the years the Supreme Court has almost entirely redefined its own role as being a supra-legislative body, and the 9th and 10th Amendments have been very nearly relegated to status of historical footnotes. Perhaps most poignant are the grander injustices – the persistence of slavery for the first nearly 90 years of the nation's independent existence, Jim Crow, and Japanese internment during WWII. So perhaps, as always, a bit of perspective is in order.

Nevertheless, it cannot be denied that something is just, well, *different* about what occurred in the wake of the pandemic. Certain phrases take hold in society during such times, repeated very nearly to the point of exhaustion; after a little while I, personally, wanted to electrocute anybody who used such phrases as "these unprecedented times." And yet, that particular phrase was about as accurate a description of the moment as any. Never before in the nation's history had we experienced the spectacle of a quasi-permanent state of emergency, with full societal lockdowns and all that accompanied them. There were, of course, institutional structures present to ostensibly deal with such major disruptions — i.e., a mechanism for declaring a state of emergency, and the executive powers and authorities which went along with that — but those had never been tested to the egregious extent to which the pandemic occasioned, and almost certainly no one had envisioned the indefinite extensions of the state of emergency. Therefore, the requisite checks and systemic corrections were not built into those orders, which virtually invited their abuse, or at least their overuse, by those for whom the functionality and power of the state is something to be embraced, not feared.

The greater concern, of course, is that abuse begets future abuse, and without major corrective surgery the temptation to utilize the vast powers granted under emergency declarations, and the correlative circumvention of traditional liberal institutions, for less legitimate purposes — i.e., the advancement of purely political ambitions — may prove too great; an entirely human temptation for which those institutions were put in place to restrain.

Let us now examine how several of those institutional tenets fared in Colorado during the COVID-19 pandemic and the other disruptions of the time period.

RULE OF LAW

The principal distinguishing feature of government in Western Civilization, and particularly in the Anglo-Saxon tradition, is the concept of the Rule of Law. The late 19th century British jurist A.V. Dicey probably best summarized the meaning of "rule of law" in his seminal 1885 tract

"Introduction to the Study of the Law of the Constitution." In characterizing the rule of law, Dicey wrote "we mean, in the first place, that no man is punishable or can be lawfully made to suffer in body or goods except for a distinct breach of law established in the ordinary legal manner before the ordinary courts of the land. In this sense the rule of law is contrasted with every system of government based on the exercise by persons in authority of wide, arbitrary, or discretionary powers of constraint."

Those two sentences cover a lot of important ground. The key phrase is "law established in the ordinary legal manner." What Dicey meant was that laws are to be made via an established, consistent, and regulated procedure; hence the development of parliamentary traditions and procedures, and those codified in the U.S. and state constitutions. He contrasts this with government run essentially by the whim of whoever is in charge. This concept is considerably more complex than can be jotted onto a bumper sticker, but is often reduced to the simple phrase, "government by law rather than by man."

This, on first blush, immediately calls into question the legitimacy of the edicts and executive orders that were churned out of the Governor's office on a nearly daily basis, including the general lockdown orders, the determination of certain categories of businesses as "essential" (and the denying of the same to others), the mask-wearing mandate, the rolling back of the time up until which bars could serve alcohol, the limits placed on size of gatherings, the restrictions on businesses and local governments when starting the reopening phase, and so on. Yet here we run into a rather fundamental difficulty; while the orders and edicts certainly were not issued in "the ordinary manner", and appeared for all the world to be "the exercise by persons in authority of wide, arbitrary, or discretionary powers of constraint," those powers and authorities, operating under the aegis of Emergency Powers, were assigned to the governor via legislative action, back in the 1990's, and promulgated "in the ordinary manner."

A legislature grants the executive branch fairly broad discretionary emergency power, under specific conditions, for a very good reason; our system of government was specifically designed by the founders to be somewhat deliberative, and resistant to rash, rapid change. In other words, government moves slowly. In times of emergency — the barbarians at the gate, or a natural disaster knocking out electricity and critical infrastructure for instance – certain decisions need to be made with greater haste than the legislative process allows. The decision to dispatch soldiers to the barricades, or to provide immediate aid and restore order, cannot be feasibly left to the constraints of democratic parliamentary deliberation. Therefore, legislative branches grant the executive a certain degree of latitude when conditions warrant the proper declaration of an emergency.

It was not anticipated that such states of emergency would resemble anything like we saw in 2020. "Emergencies", as envisioned by the lawmakers who drafted the emergency powers bills, were generally perceived to be acute, and of short duration, often somewhat localized. The 9-11 attacks, or the 2013 floods come to mind. No one anticipated a scenario where a declared state of emergency drew out into months, and the executive actions emanating from the declaration extending over virtually every aspect of social and economic life. Nor did they anticipate that the state of emergency would be simply renewed and extended every 30 days.

To be sure, the pandemic prompted emergency declarations to be announced in every state of the union. But it was interesting to observe how that played out in each state. Befitting our federalist system, each state legislature granted executive emergency powers a little differently. For instance, early in May, the Wisconsin Supreme Court struck down the "safer at home" orders issued by Gov. Tony Evers, since the emergency powers law in that state did not grant the governor the leeway to do such things unilaterally. Other states, notably California (to no one's surprise), go the other way, and have bestowed in statute emergency powers to the governor that would make King George III envious. Colorado's lie somewhere in the middle.

What was perhaps more telling was the difference in manner of utilizing those powers, between Democratic and Republican governors. Generally speaking, Republican governors exercised their authority with considerably more economy and restraint, granting more flexibility and decision making authority to local governments, resisting statewide mandates, being less draconian in terms of lockdowns, and quicker to allow commerce to restart. By contrast, Democratic governors tended to make full use of their newfound authority, issuing sweeping statewide mandates and edicts, eagerly shutting down society (and for a longer period of time), and generally micromanaging the response. Tales of the arbitrary and absurd nature of some of the orders became the stuff of legend; like Michigan's banning motor boats and seed sales, and the report in Hawaii of how the Maui Brewing Company, which had good naturedly shifted its production to hand sanitizer as its part in the crisis, was investigated by the Department of Liquor Control for the heinous act of giving away some of the excess sanitizer with a purchase.

Colorado, for the most part, avoided some of the most egregious of these scenarios, but the state exhibited plenty of examples to illustrate the arbitrary nature of the executive orders under which its citizens lived for weeks:

- the announcement that liquor stores were to be shut down, as they represented too great of a risk for close contact — initiating a (somehow unforeseen) run on liquor stores which prompted the state to decide, magically, that they were, in fact essential services after all;
- enforcement against a Hobby Lobby, which had kept its doors open due to the fact that it sold, among other useful stay-at-home items, material from which to manufacture face masks — while down the street Home Depot was allowed to remain open to sell lumber and lawnmowers;
- the very fact that marijuana shops were considered "essential", but churches were not;
- and of course — there was the scene which made national news of local police handcuffing a father in front of his young daughter on a playground for the heinous offence of playing catch in violation of Stay-at-Home orders.

Around the nation, the occurrence of these sorts of incidents seemed to correspond inversely with how heavy the hand was on the government tiller; and that hand was heavier in states governed by those whose philosophical inclinations were disposed towards embracing the functionality of government as a solution for everything. Colorado was no exception to this.

SEPARATION OF POWERS

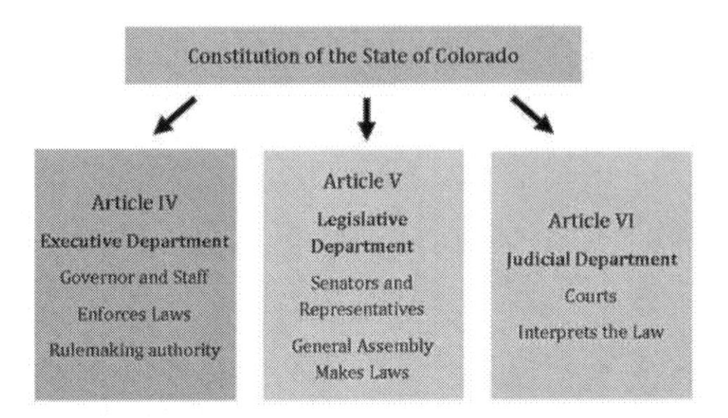

Between March and August of 2020, the state of Colorado lived under executive branch edict. Governor Polis issued over 170 executive orders, which covered just about every facet of social and economic life one could imagine, and it is an exceedingly difficult task to try and make the argument that he did not overstep his authority and overuse the emergency powers he was granted. But it is also impossible to lay all the blame entirely on him. The same statute which grants him those powers includes this line: "The general assembly, by joint resolution, may terminate a state of disaster emergency at any time. Thereupon, the governor shall issue an executive order or proclamation ending the state of disaster emergency."

In other words, the legislative branch could have, at any time it wanted, revoked the governor's emergency authority and reclaimed its own authority to make laws "in the ordinary manner." That would have provided the opportunity for the legislative chambers to debate the various measures employed to respond to the pandemic, including the various layers of economic lockdown. More public scrutiny would have been afforded to those measures, and a wider range of necessary input offered, such as that of the business community. At the very least, it would have granted a degree of legitimacy that was missing in the law being generated by executive order.

Unfortunately, that did not happen. With a Democratic majority holding both chambers, a resolution never got to the floor. A proposed joint Resolution was, in fact, drafted and introduced in the Senate by Sen. Rob Woodward (R-Loveland), but was killed in committee on a party-line vote. There was nary a whisper from Democratic leadership supporting a move to reclaim oversight and lawmaking authority. Thus, in effect, the majority in both chambers gave tacit approval to being sidelined and ignored.

Rather strangely, this attitude of passivity in the face of executive power held even when it came to disbursing federal funding that was provided to the state in the first round of COVID-19 relief, under the federal CARES Act. The legislature, which ordinarily guards jealously its power of the purse, was not even consulted as Governor Polis distributed $1.6 billion in CARES money, magnanimously giving the legislature 4% of the federal funds to appropriate in the normal manner.

Now, of course, this can be partially explained by politics; Democratic lawmakers had no particular desire or incentive to publicly challenge a Democratic governor, especially in an election year. But it also speaks to a philosophical element; the Democratic Party has traditionally (at least for the past century or so) been in favor of the centralization of power. Notwithstanding the recent fetish for "local control" of such things as oil and gas development and pesticide use – employed only on issues that a) truly are a state-level concern, b) economic and scientific reality prohibits statewide adoption of the desired policy, and c) since they *are* legitimately state-wide concerns, "local control" equates to de-facto state policy – the political left, as embodied in the U.S. by the Democratic Party, has advocated for a steady centralization of power, over, for instance, education, healthcare, housing, economic regulation, and so on. It ought to come as no surprise that they embrace so fully the weight of governing authority being placed in the most central location there is.

PROPER ROLE OF GOVERNMENT

The wholly unprecedented elongation of a statewide emergency declaration, and the wanton use of unilateral executive power amid legislative silence, would be bad enough on their own, had the pandemic been the only catalytic element at play. The state reaction to the civil unrest that broke out in the wake of the killing of George Floyd in police custody in Minneapolis, highlighted what may be an even deeper malady afflicting liberal governance in the state.

The protests, while ostensibly about perceived racial

injustice, quickly took on an ideological, violent tone and devolved into vandalism, violence, and rioting. Businesses throughout the downtown area were damaged, dozens of police officers were injured (some severely), in some cases restaurant workers were forced to barricade themselves in their stores until police could rescue them hours later, and the State Capitol – the very symbol of liberal democracy and civil life as lived in Colorado – was vandalized. Every window within range of a bat or rock was shattered, exceedingly vulgar graffiti was spray painted everywhere the guttersnipes could reach, monuments to veterans and other heroes of our society were defaced, and even the statue of a civil-war era Union soldier — fighting to end slavery — was torn down. Buildings for several blocks around the capitol were boarded up for weeks, as the violence continued, night after night.

The reaction of the governor, whose primary job is to ensure public safety and order, was, to say the least, underwhelming. Far too few State Patrol troopers were present to protect the Capitol, and the Governor did nothing to ensure the meager force normally on hand was backed up by sufficient numbers from other jurisdictions, which was within his power to do. He did issue a call to mobilize the National Guard; but if they were deployed, no one knows quite where or what they were doing. Certainly, ARNG (Army National Guard) combat engineers could have quickly erected barricades around the Capitol and other state buildings to protect them. Despite the extensive damage, the injuries to police officers, the fires, and even the gunshots fired at the Capitol on the first day (possibly directed at two Democratic lawmakers), few arrests were made and fewer still prosecutions or convictions.

What was stunning was the inaction of the governor's office

in the face of weeks of street violence and civil disturbance, juxtaposed with the over-ambition of the previous two and half months. Governor Polis was more than happy to utilize his emergency power to anoint certain businesses as "essential" and order others to remain locked, suspend rent payments, grant or disapprove county re-opening plans with a thumb-up-or-down like Caesar, distribute $1.6 billion in federal relief funds on his own accord, and issue almost daily executive orders; but when it came time to rightfully use those powers he was given to perform his primary duty of restoring law and order on the streets, his approach became instantly *laissez faire.*

Governments are established to provide order in an unordered world. In the Western, and particularly the American tradition, governments are put in place to secure their citizens in their liberty – order is a prerequisite for liberty, and it is the role of government to use the authority given to them by the people to safeguard their freedom and property. James Madison famously wrote in *Federalist 51*, "If men were angels, no government would be necessary."

Alexander Hamilton warned in the same document that if government abdicates this responsibility to uphold order, then "we shall be obliged to conclude that the United States will afford the extraordinary spectacle of a government destitute even of the shadow of constitutional power to enforce the execution of its own laws." *The failure of the government to fulfill its central duty while simultaneously overextending itself in other areas betrays a confusion among the American Left of what the role of government actually is, a confusion that turns the purpose of government on its head, and bears serious consequences for our future.*

CONCLUSION

What are those consequences? First, in the near term, is the economic damage that will be wrought by prolonged societal shutdown. Some economic harm in the face of the pandemic was unavoidable; but the degree will differ among jurisdictions. One of the beauties of the American system of federalist government is that subsidiary invites innovations of approach; in other words, in times like we saw with the COVID-19 pandemic, the entire nation is not consigned to a blanket approach which may prove wrong. How much greater would be the death toll, one wonders, if Governor Cuomo's approach were applied nationally? It will be some time yet before the full picture emerges of how effective or prudent each state's response was; but it is almost certain that those states which applied a lighter touch will recover sooner, and more fully, than those which exercised a more iron grip. While hindsight is always an unfair test, Coloradans will be asking for some time whether a less authoritarian application would have created a better economic climate than that we are now suffering.

The second major consequence relates to the failure of government to do its real duty. Already crime rates are soaring in Denver, as they are in other cities which failed to retake control of their streets from anarchic ideologues. The rhetorical narcotic which has gripped not only Democratic politicians, academia, and the media, but that has wafted down to corporate America and professional sports, and which is lively in the Denver City Council, School Board, and parts of the legislature, is undoing many of the reforms of the 1990's and early 2000's which served to reduce crime rates and make the streets safe. We strongly risk a return to the days of the 1970's and early 1980's, where the inner cities were virtually unlivable. Public opinion and outrage will demand that particular pendulum swing back, but how many lives will be ruined before we get there?

The third consequence will be more abstract, but no less important. The systematic damage to our political institutions, if not irreversible, is severe. Many of the governing edifices that were put in place over generations to protect from the type of arbitrary and tyrannical abuses that threaten any society, were summarily cast aside by the governing authorities — the Governor and the Democrat majority in the legislature — during the pandemic for the sake of expediency. We saw power shift, virtually overnight, from the legislature to the executive, and from the constitution as the basis of law to the courts, as determiner, not interpreter, of law.

And the ultimate risk, of course, is of future abuse. Once a restraining structure is broken, it becomes more difficult to put it back in place. The excesses observed in 2020 may have been for a legitimate cause, the curbing of a public health crisis. But will it enable similar excesses to occur at a future date, in the name of handling a proclaimed climate emergency, or a declared social justice emergency?

History would suggest that such abuses are not so remote as we might hope — which is why Madison included the second part of his famous quote in *Federalist 51:* “If angels were to govern men, neither external nor internal controls on government would be necessary.”

4

THE DEMOCRATS $30 BILLION BUDGET IS UNSUSTAINABLE, AND THEY KNOW IT

BY KIM RANSOM
Colorado State Representative

In November of 2018, when Democrats won a majority in the State Senate after four years of a Republican Senate majority, the ratio on the General Assembly's Joint Budget Committee changed from 3-3 and became a 4-2 Democrat majority. This meant that the budget would no longer be truly bi-partisan, since the four Democrats could win any motion to adopt a line item.

Elections do indeed have consequences, and sometimes the consequences are swift in coming.

The annual Colorado state government budget is drafted by the six members of the Joint Budget Committee (JBC), with professional support from the non-partisan staff. The six legislators are comprised of three Senators and three Representatives, two from the majority party and one from the minority in each camber. When one house is controlled by Democrats and the other by Republicans, this creates a 3-3 balance in the Joint Budget Committee, or JBC as it's commonly referred to. Whether the majority is by one seat, ten seats, or more, the makeup and number of JBC members for each chamber remains the same, six. So even in recent years when the Senate had a thin majority of 18-17 and the House had a wider majority of 37-28, the Joint Budget Committee was still evenly split with three Republicans and three Democrats, giving meaning and clarity to the phrase, "Majorities Matter."

The total state budget has been growing drastically, due to multiple factors. First, the population in Colorado grows each year as more and more people have seen the beauty of our state and the wonderful way of life that exists here. The Taxpayers' Bill of Rights and our "flat tax" have created a favorable atmosphere for businesses and entrepreneurs to operate and prosper. There are other factors leading to budget growth as well, including the increased federal dollars associated with the Affordable Care Act and the Medicaid expansion, adopted in 2013 when the Democrats were previously in control of both chambers and the governorship.

In June of 2020, after six months of JBC deliberations interrupted by a mid-March to end of May recess resulting from concerns generated by the COVID-19 pandemic, the $30 billion state budget was passed by Democrat majorities in the House and Senate and then signed by the Governor. What neither the Governor nor the General Assembly's Democrat leadership admitted or bothered to point out, however, is that the budget adopted by unanimous vote of all 60 Democrats in the General Assembly was neither "balanced" nor sustainable. In fact, looking ahead to the 2021-22 fiscal year, we're headed into a train wreck.

Why did not a single Republican in the state House of Representatives vote for this budget? Well, we can start with the fact that it is in "balance" only by a charitable definition of balance. The existence of even one dollar in the statutory Reserve — or a credible *estimate* of one dollar remaining in the Reserve at the end of the fiscal year — signals an excess of Revenue over Appropriations. Thus, by definition, the budget is in balance if ANY Reserve exists in the budget bill enacted more than a year ahead of the end of the fiscal year. No Democrat member of the JBC went to the microphone on the floor of the House of Representatives during the debate on the budget bill (traditionally called the "Long Bill" because no other piece of legislation can compete with its 600-plus pages) to point out that between the day the budget bill was first introduced (May 25) and the final vote (June 15), that the "Reserve" was decreased *twice*.

To further complicate the issue, the Reserve designated in the Long Bill is only an estimate based on another estimate, the financial forecast adopted by the Joint Budget

Committee based on what amounts to our state economists' best guess on likely fiscal year tax receipts. Each quarter, two economic forecasts are presented, and during the budget balancing process, one of the two is chosen as the benchmark. Traditionally, the Joint Budget Committee has chosen the more conservative budget, the one with the lower revenue forecast, which would help allow for a margin of error in the forecasts. But for the 2020/21 budget year, the less conservative — or slightly more optimistic — forecast was chosen with the understanding that the "extra" amount of approximately $437M would be held in the statutory reserve.

After being introduced, the budget moved through the legislative process, and the legislated statutory reserve was reduced by $100 million. There were three weeks between the Long Bill's introduction on May 25 and its final adoption on June 15. The Joint Budget Committee sponsor was obligated to amend the bill establishing the statutory reserve, HB20-1383, on the floor of the Senate only two days prior to adoption of the Long Bill. The reserve dropped from 3.84% to 2.86% . Keep in mind, the prior budget year had a reserve of 7.25%. The $100M of the "extra" agreed-to reserve was eaten away by amendments to the budget in the House and the Senate, as well as new bills that were passed. Single party control of the legislature allowed this to proceed without the checks and balances that additional input might have offered.

There are many other reasons for Republican skepticism about the budget crafted by the Democrat majorities and sent to Governor Polis. The most serious flaw in the Democrats' 2020/2021 budget is that similar budget reductions are simply not available in the troubled years immediately ahead. Put simply in dollar terms, the majority of the spending reductions used to achieve a balanced budget were one-time cuts that cannot be duplicated in subsequent budgets. Dozens of accumulated cash funds raided in order to move huge amounts into the General Fund for "balancing" are now depleted.

But the vanishing cash funds are only the tip of the iceberg. It gets worse.

The postponement of the scheduled PERA direct contribution in order to save $225 million theoretically could be repeated, but it is universally agreed that would be extremely irresponsible, with risky and irreversible long-term consequences. Colorado's public employee retirement system, like many other state retirement funds, has a serious long-term solvency problem that has been building for many years. Bipartisan legislation enacted in 2018 commits the legislature to an annual direct contribution that cannot be perpetually kicked down the road. The obligation to retirees is just that – an obligation, a debt that is owed after their career in state government. These retirees spent their careers paying into the PERA system rather than into Social Security, so most are not eligible for Social Security. While they may have their own savings, or be able to continue working, they have been counting on their PERA retirement benefits. An insolvent system would have a hugely detrimental effect on both retirees and current employees, as well as hurt Colorado's credit rating.

Some other large reductions in the FY2021 budget, like the downsizing of state Corrections facilities, are based on optimistic assumptions about the "caseload" that may not materialize. This assumption is dependent on the judicial system and the courts. With rising crime rates in Denver and elsewhere, the caseload may in fact increase.

In addition, many of the "balancing bills" used by the Democrat majority over Republican opposition in the final weeks of the legislative session are also one-time "fixes" that cannot be duplicated next year or in subsequent years.

Another point to keep in mind is that the Colorado state budget uses the practice of "baseline based" budgeting, as opposed to beginning with a "zero base." For those not familiar with those terms, a "zero-based budget" means that the JBC would be able to examine a department's entire operating budget from ground zero, whereas a baseline budget is presented with last year's budget as the baseline – the starting point – and the JBC only seriously considers the additional add-on line items and percentage increases requested for the upcoming year. While extra effort would be required at the front end in the agencies' submissions, a zero-based approach requires both the JBC and each department to truly examine and justify *all* of their spending patterns, not just proposed increases.

As it stands now, once the legislature approves – and the governor signs — a budget, each line item falls into the abyss of last year's appropriation. This approach may come back to haunt us in the deliberations over the next budget, if businesses remain closed or unable to fully recover quickly. Decreasing revenue means the size of the government budget will need to — as it should - decrease right along with the overall economy. However, progressives are full of stratagems and magical nostrums to avoid any proportionate downsizing in government, maneuvers like creating new "fees" and "enterprises" that are really tax increases in disguise.

Thankfully for taxpayers, there is still some accountability. Luckily we have a State Auditor that conducts thorough audits of departments periodically, and the Director of each department reports to the elected Governor. Directors give a presentation (commonly referred to as a SMART Act hearing) to one or more committees of reference early in each legislative session, in which committee members are allowed to ask questions about agency performance and management. However, it's not enough.

This baseline budgeting system encourages the legislature to debate the minutia – the new budget requests – while the existing budget (including the ever-growing number of employees, or FTE) is barely examined. In recent years the state budget has grown approximately $1 billion/year – yes, that's billion with a "b" – and the number of state employees has grown right along with it.

In the preceding four fiscal years, 2017 to 2020, twelve of eighteen agencies experienced total appropriation increases averaging above five percent annually, almost three times the average population increases in those years, and several had average annual appropriations growth above ten percent.

In 2020, there were two bills passed that will send referred measures to the ballot in November in an effort to increase taxes on Coloradans. Thankfully, the Taxpayer Bill of Rights, adopted by the voters in 1992, is still in the state Constitution and still in effect. This Bill of Rights prevents the majority party from simply raising tax rates, or adopting new taxes by the vote of the legislature. It means that the legislature needs to ask the voters for a tax increase, and describe what the increase will be used for, giving real meaning to the phrase ". . . . with the consent of the governed."

A proposed new tax on tobacco and nicotine products must

go to the voters for approval in November, and while technically not a part of the balancing formula for the coming fiscal year, it illuminates a dysfunctional characteristic of Democrat fiscal policy: the irresistible impulse to create new long-term spending obligations even in the midst of an unprecedented financial crisis. Typically, the price tag for any new program is modest the first year and then grows substantially in the "out years." (But, hey: that will be someone else's budget problem years from now; wink-wink.)

The voters of Colorado have let us know over and over at the ballot box that they expect us to work without raising taxes unless they approve yet another increase. We can increase the budget as population and inflation grow, which we do. In fact, the budget has been growing far in excess of the allowed formula, as legislators vote to move monies into TABOR exempt enterprises and also to add ever-increasing fees to many of the services that citizens need and expect from state government. The Taxpayer Bill of Rights gives the legislature a much needed curb which prevents us from increasing tax rates to spend money on new programs that many Coloradans may or may not want.

The Next Budget: Where will the money come from?

Democrat leadership knows all of this; they recognize and admit that the approach to next year's budget must be different. But, how different, exactly? Are there any clues to their plans?

The Democrats' strategy for balancing the FY2021/22 budget appears to be based on political assumptions which are "optimistic" — and highly problematic. What ties them all together is the missing commitment to the most neglected part of the just-adopted budget: a lack of serious attention to the challenge of economic recovery.

Unlike Democrats, Republicans recognize the folk wisdom in the saying, when you find yourself in a hole, first, stop digging. The Democrats' budget does next to nothing to reduce barriers to job creation and economic recovery. Quite the contrary: Democrats look to tax increases — and new "fees" — as a solution to downstream budget deficits.

Another strategy we will likely see from the majority party for balancing the next budget boils down to lobbying the federal government for the next rescue installment. They are demanding the next federal bailout include the "flexibility" to backfill lost revenue. Democrats are already working overtime to generate public demand for another three-trillion dollar federal bailout, which you might call budget balancing by proxy. Uncle Sam has "deep pockets," haven't you heard? Of course, they're leaving out the fact that Colorado taxpayers pay federal taxes, too. Our children, grandchildren, and even great-grandchildren will likely be paying off the federal deficits that already exist.

Is there a backup plan in the Democrats' back pocket? Of course. When all else fails, when your political allies will not let you take on the task of a genuine restructuring of the baseline costs of state government, then blame the "budget crisis" on the Taxpayers Bill of Rights and demand an emergency tax increase. They want to ignore the explicit prohibition in TABOR against tax increases based primarily on revenue shortfalls. There was also a new proposal to switch from Colorado's flat tax system to a progressive income tax resembling the tax system in the liberal state to our west, California. (Thankfully, the proposed initiative to accomplish that change through a November ballot measure fell flat, and was abandoned).

The 100 elected lawmakers of the 73rd General Assembly who convene on January 13, 2021 will choose one of two paths to economic recovery and fiscal health and accountability. Regretfully, Democrats have no plan, and frankly, no desire to achieve a balanced budget through economic growth. Republicans do have a plan, and it begins with the maxim, *stop digging a deeper hole!*

We can balance the budget by honest, forthright prioritization of the legitimate functions of state government most important to all Coloradans. We will give top priority to elements in the budget that fall within the proper role of government, which will lead to job creation, economic growth, and a robust recovery. Front and center we will find areas of waste, along with areas that have increased efficiencies over time (computers, anyone?).

Republicans also want the legislature to take much more seriously its constitutional duty to provide meaningful oversight of state agency rule-making, which often imposes undue burdens on citizens and businesses far beyond what was contemplated in legislation. And as argued in one of the other chapters of this book, the legislature must stop enacting laws that give overly broad and ill-defined rule-making powers to unaccountable bureaucracies and independent commissions. Such legislation amounts to an unconstitutional delegation of lawmaking authority to an administrative body.

The legislature must also take seriously the threat to its appropriations authority displayed by Governor Polis' unilateral capture and allocation of $1.6 billion in federal pandemic relief funding, while leaving only 4% of the federal funds to the authority of the legislature. Even if the JBC agrees with the Governor's allocations, those decisions should be weighed in committee and approved in the chambers of the General Assembly, not in the Governor's office.

Such actions would allow Colorado's elected lawmakers to maintain the current level of taxation and still provide the essential services needed and expected by the people of Colorado, even in periods of hardship. Effective, responsible government is above all government that respects the constitutional rights and liberties of all Coloradans.

Part Two: You Won't Believe What They Did Today

How long, LORD, must I call for help, but you do not listen? Or cry out to you, "Violence!" but you do not save? Why do you make me look at injustice?

Why do you tolerate wrongdoing? Destruction and violence are before me; there is strife, and conflict abounds.

Therefore the law is paralyzed, and justice never prevails. The wicked hem in the righteous, so that justice is perverted.

Habakkuk 1:2-4

5

WHERE'S JARED? CAPITOL SECURITY TAKES A KNEE

BY GRAY BUCKLEY
Law Enforcement Specialist

In the spring of 2020, Coloradoans watched their Capitol being attacked and its building and grounds trashed while police were nowhere to be seen. Where were the Denver police? Where was the Colorado State Patrol, which by statute has the authority to enforce the law on state property and grounds? And who pays for the millions of dollars in damage?

Many Coloradans are justifiably wondering: if mobs of "protestors" can do this to the State Capitol and nearby private property under the nose of the Governor and elected lawmakers, is anyone safe?

The Capitol symbolizes the majesty of Colorado, its land and people. An attack on the Capitol is a crime, not only against property, but against all it represents. Unless the law protects the people who obey it and punishes those who break it, Colorado is doomed. Elected officials cowering from predators and leaving State property and records unprotected are yielding to mob rule, forsaking their oaths, and turning their backs on taxpaying citizens. That is gross nonfeasance or malfeasance, or both.

"The Rule of Law in its simplest form . . . means that 'no one is above the law.'

> *It is the foundation for the development of peaceful, equitable and prosperous societies. For the rule of law to be effective, there must be equality under the law, transparency of law, an independent judiciary and access to legal remedy."*
> — LexisNexis

Fundamental Responsibility

Our Colorado Constitution was ratified to ". . . establish justice; insure tranquility." It says that each of us has "natural, essential and inalienable rights, among which may be reckoned the right of enjoying and defending . . . lives and liberties; of . . . possessing and protecting property . . ." One of the Governor's primary duties is to "take care that the laws be faithfully executed." The Governor has the constitutionally assigned "power to call out the militia to execute the laws, suppress insurrection or repel invasion."

Reinforcing our natural and inalienable rights, the 14th Amendment to the United States Constitution says in part, ". . . No State shall deny to any person within its jurisdiction the equal protection of the laws." Consistent with authority memorialized in our Constitutions, there are laws that prohibit and penalize theft, vandalism, burglary, assault, arson and riot. It is the duty of elected officials and law enforcement officers to enforce those laws in order for each of us to enjoy life, liberty and peace.

The first priority of government is the defense of its people. When executive officials forsake that duty, the credibility of government and public confidence in government is reduced. The public's fear of crime is understandably increased and their quality of life decreased is proportionately.

What is the real story here?

Why were these well-founded and well understood principles ignored and even denigrated in Colorado during civil disorders in May and June and extending well into July? Why did the Denver Police chief issue a "stand down, do not interfere" order to police officers during a pro-police "6th Annual Law Enforcement Appreciation Day " rally at Civic Center Park on July 19 ? Two hundred citizens with a rally permit were violently attacked by a mob of over 400 anti-police rioters while police did nothing to halt the attacks and protect individuals being assaulted.

No, this is not about people assembling peaceably for the common good and then going on their way afterwards. It is a story of riot and assault upon our way of life, an assault upon liberty and justice, and sadly, also a story of elected officials who cower when challenged by riotous, rampaging mobs who attack and destroy public and private property. It is also the story of a small, well organized group of people, many of them Marxists and anarchists, who wish to overthrow the government of the United States and forcefully establish a new society.

Who abandoned their posts, or did not know their duty, or who willingly ignored their duty? The recent riotous and flagrantly criminal behavior that went largely uninterrupted suggests that elected officials were either (a) caught off guard; (b) were ill-prepared for decision making during calamitous events; or (c) that they interfered either incompetently, carelessly or deliberately with efforts to preserve the peace.

During these events, did the Governor and Denver's mayor consult appropriately with their peers and with federal disaster/planning agencies? Did our leaders consult with others and then ignore good advice? From all reports, the Governor of Colorado was both silent and AWOL at the end of May during the week of ongoing nightly rampages, even as his first-floor office in the Capitol was targeted for window smashing and obscene graffiti.

Speaking of the Governor of the Centennial State, why did he wait nearly two months after the May rioting before officially asking the City of Denver to grant the Colorado State Patrol authority to issue citations and warrants *for crimes they observe being committed on the Capitol grounds, which is state property?* The State Patrol has had that authority in every other city and county in the state, in 63 counties, but not in Denver — which just happens to be the location of the State Capitol and Supreme Court and the headquarters of every state agency.

Have some Colorado policy making officials interfered with operational decisions at the State and local levels the way the Mayor of Baltimore did not long ago when she told the police commissioner (and thus his officers), to ignore hundreds of felony crimes in progress — because it was 'just property'? Following tradition and training, Denver Police and the State Patrol followed operational policy direction from their agency leadership rather than attend directly to their sworn duty to protect life and property, to arrest violators, and to preserve the peace. The responsibility for the "do not interfere" orders rests almost entirely on elected officials, not police commanders.

For the police, dispersing disorderly crowds and unlawful assemblies, and arresting people for crimes committed in their presence, is not 22nd Century police science. Neither is it rocket science. We watched as businesses threatened or destroyed by rioters have closed for good. Jobs have been lost. Sales tax revenues have dropped, and fiscal support for vital public services has been threatened. At best this is the cost of neglect. Why do we tolerate leaders who order police not to interfere with the destruction of millions of dollars worth of private and/or public property? Fire fighters are never ordered to stop fighting fires that only threaten property. Why the police?

Administrative Questions & Political Answers

Do we expect law enforcement to follow unlawful orders? What do we expect law enforcement to do if given unlawful orders? Are Colorado law enforcement agencies derelict when they fail to stop felony crimes that happen in front of them? Can they be sued?

These are not difficult questions, though discussion may be awkward and troubling. But discussion is necessary for there to be accountability and community stability.

Citizens do not expect their government to fail, especially not in full view of television cameras. People do not want to believe the unpleasant things they see: In the United States systemic failures involving mob behavior are neither frequent nor acceptable. Broadcasting Colorado leadership's malfeasance to the nation does not encourage healthy economic development or investment in Colorado industry.

Lately we are seeing Internet ads inviting 'protesters' and 'demonstrators' to show up at designated times and places to demonstrate 'peacefully' — *for pay* — with bottles, bricks, clubs, and an assortment of crude weapons. We watch and listen to network and local news commentators describe the physical attacks on innocent citizens as 'mostly peaceful' protests. Millions of dollars of damage have been inflicted on the Colorado Capitol, on patrol cars, on officers, and on private businesses while, under orders, normally dutiful police have had to stand... and watch.

Official Nonfeasance — the Consequences

For many days mob rule prevailed in the heart of Denver. The police chief diverted hundreds of police officers from other parts of Denver to stand and watch while rioters damaged and destroyed property around a six-block area adjacent to the Capitol Complex. The adjacent state Supreme Court building had to be fenced off to protect it from additional onslaughts. Loss estimates range to millions of dollars, and state agencies are being suspiciously slow to tally all the costs. Is that because, in the words of one Colorado State Patrol officer at the end of June, "It's not over"?

Television viewers, and innocent citizens caught in the fray, likely concluded that government was either incapable or unwilling to restore order. Citizens in the rest of Denver were left with fewer defenders. Business owners, already suffering COVID-19-related economic loss, feared losing their businesses altogether as mobs danced in the street, smashed windows, and looted stores.

Colorado business owners and taxpayers were unjustly penalized as emergency service resources were held in ready reserve in downtown Denver. Thus, the rest of the city was deprived of more timely response in time of need. And yet, oddly, those available resources were not utilized to stop or apprehend those who were damaging property and threatening both police and innocent bystanders.

Will the rule of law prevail in Colorado? Has a precedent been set? Is it alright now in Denver to burn and to destroy private property? Calling it a slippery slope is an understatement, and there is more at stake than economic stability and recovery. What is at stake is the civic order and public respect for government authority.

Allegedly motivated by the death of George Floyd in Minneapolis, a black man who died in police custody, mobs directed their professionally organized fury against every law enforcement officer in the nation. And by their deliberate inaction and misconduct, many elected officials neglected their sworn duty and stood, not for the rule of law, but for enabling systematic violence that threatens more than life and property.

A Duty to Serve the Law

When well organized riots began in late May, seeded by well intentioned people who believed carrying street signs in a parade would lead to the eradication of police brutality, a well organized cadre of admitted Marxist and anarchists began depredation and criminal assaults. Their admitted intent is to overthrow the government of the United States, the government of the States, and the government of cities and towns. But first, they intend to eliminate law enforcement.

One of their frequent slogans is, "No justice, no peace," which translates to, "surrender to our demands or face unrelenting violence." The intelligent observer knows that without obedience to law there will be neither justice nor peace. Defunding the police is a recipe for rule by the mob with the biggest bullhorn and the most bricks and baseball bats.

Peace officers sworn to enforce the law and to support and defend our constitutional guarantees are waiting for permission to do their duty. The police are standing ready to enforce the law every minute, every hour and every day. They answer calls for help every hour of the day and the people working nine to five, Monday to Friday, expect the same. Without asking or waiting for permission, the police protect us all from thieves and worse. Inexplicably, Denver police were not authorized or directed to protect Colorado's Capitol when it was under direct attack.

We have seen what happens when public officials either forget their oaths, or are hesitant to or incapable of doing their jobs. Continuing riots in Denver (and now Aurora) and attacks on peaceful assemblies are examples. Absent responsible, faithful leadership, disorder will continue until government falls in disarray. And that is precisely the objective of the organizers and financial backers of recent attacks on civil authority in Colorado.

For Years Denver Refused to Help Protect the State Capitol

Until late July of 2020, unlike the governments of every other Colorado home rule city, the Denver Mayor and City Council would not authorize the State Patrol to enforce municipal ordinances concerning ordinary crimes against property. Denver's County Attorney would not accept case filings from the State Patrol unless those charges/arrests had been approved by the Denver Police. Inexplicably that 'permission' was withheld for years until weeks of violent disorder and public property vandalism on the Capitol grounds generated a public outcry.

For weeks the Governor of Colorado remained silent on the matter of Colorado State Patrol's arrest authority. He waited weeks after the riots began before finally — after a direct appeal from former Republican Governor Bill Owens — asking Denver to change its policy.

No Police, No Law — The New Order

Admitted Marxists in Denver are working to eliminate the police and to replace officers with specialists not obliged or paid to make arrests or to stop crime. There will be burning, looting, criminal assaults on businesses, the elderly, and the infirm. Without publicly funded law enforcement, citizens who witness crimes will be on their own to detain criminals, and will have no jail to hold them. Vigilante justice will replace law enforcement and unofficial justice will be administered quickly and sometimes unjustly. The street radicals will cheer the escalating disorder.

Part of the Marxists' "Defund the Police" initiative in dozens of cities is to increase funding for "civic specialists" or "social support staff" to take over emergency response duties from the police. Emergency phone calls would not be taken by police or fire personnel, but would be answered in a screening center (as they are today), similar to triage in a hospital emergency room.

In the new Emergency Call Center system, with police personnel replaced by social workers and mental health specialists, Call Takers would learn from a caller(s) the nature and extent of the incident(s) being reported, with property crimes assigned the lowest priority for response,

At any urban call center, sometimes dozens of calls arrive within seconds about the same event. Operators must coordinate their call handling (as they do today) before the appropriate responder is notified. But, due to the reallocation of duties to enlarged or newly created assistance agencies, the call takers will need to know more than whether to send police, paramedics, or fire fighters. Based on the information conveyed to the call taker, a decision(s) will be required; i.e., who will we send and when? The mind boggles at the exponential loss of life and property as police dispatchers are replaced by crisis managers and social workers, and the response to call for help are prioritized according to the political character and "social justice" merit of the incident.

Diverting Police Funds

There is already keen competition for public funds among multiple public service agencies. The majority of the State budget is allocated to other than law enforcement and public safety services. In the Fiscal Year 2019-2020 Colorado State budget, no more than 9% is appropriated for public safety, including corrections and judicial. When we exclude corrections and judicial expenditures, that drops to less than 3%. How much lower can public safety go in the era of the "New Normal"? We may soon find out.

As public safety funds are diverted/reduced/defunded, there will be a reduction in resources to conduct crime and traffic investigations. Some local prosecutors already refuse to prosecute crimes of theft where the loss is $500 or less, thereby effectively pardoning all such offenses (a power properly reserved for the governor). Some agencies will not conduct investigations of motor vehicle theft, regardless of loss value, instead inviting victims to fill out an electronic report or to visit the station and to complete a report of their own. This gives auto thieves extra time to re-sell or part-out their loot. These protocols are policy based rather than fiscally impractical.

Because many police agencies are insufficiently staffed, some crime and crash victims wait for hours, if not days, before assistance arrives for an on scene investigation.

Potentially life threatening events take priority over investigations of newly discovered crimes that happened hours or days ago. Some agencies regularly delay response even to life threatening events because available officers are attending other violent crime and crash calls. Diverting funds from these response services will further render rescue and enforcement services less effective. Lives will be lost unnecessarily.

Constitutional and statutory provisions provide reasonably clear guidelines for the conduct of both government institutions and a civil society. Respect for the law in those documents, and obedience to law, are the foundations of a free society. Surely, the respect for law begins with respect for the building and institution where the people's democratically elected representatives meet to debate, deliberate and vote on the laws which protect and defend "equal justice under law."

Until now, that respect for law was largely taken for granted and enforced in a nonpartisan manner by responsible officials.

6

COLORADO'S ARROGANT, POLITICIZED PUBLIC HEALTH BUREAUCRACY

BY KEVIN LUNDBERG
Former Colorado State Senator

I don't trust public health bureaucrats. They taught me not to.

In early March, when the COVID-19 pandemic was just starting to spread in the U.S., I commented to a good friend, who is a medical doctor, that one outcome of this epidemic would be that public health would lose a great deal of credibility. I based this statement on my experience as a legislator dealing with the public health department over the past decades.

Before my tenure in the Colorado legislature, I served on the Colorado Commission for Family Medicine. Then, during my 16 years in the legislature, I served for 14 years on health committees, including as chair for the Senate committee. This experience gave me repeated opportunities for dealing with officials from the Colorado Department of Public Health and Environment (CDPHE). It became obvious, very quickly, that these trained scientists, many of whom were medical doctors, had traded in their objective, scientific professionalism for something more like the role of a propaganda specialist.

I am certain that these men and women started their careers with the idea of helping people and fighting disease. However, in their rush to persuade people to follow their directions, they became very adept at bending the truth to support their immediate goals. We like to think that public health is driven strictly by facts and proven theories, but the reality is much different.

The command and control policies everyone has seen during this pandemic may be surprising to some, but it is actually quite consistent with their long-term patterns. As we explore the policies and history of CDPHE in this chapter, we shall discover that, without more checks and balances to their power, these unelected government bureaucrats are in charge of far too much of our daily lives.

And before we dive into their recent history, don't forget their next big project; in July of this year, they declared racism is a mental health crisis.[1] Never let a crisis go to waste. And if you don't have a crisis, make one up.

There are some residual racist attitudes toward minority groups in Colorado, but for those of us who can look back for a half-century or more, we have come a long way in correcting these problems. After examining CDPHE's track record we will see that whenever they get involved in a major state policy they milk it for all the power and control they can gather.

CDPHE's "cure" will probably be far more dangerous than the crisis they claim to be addressing.

Asbestos

One of my first encounters with CDPHE concerned asbestos. I was first elected to the Colorado House of Representatives in 2002, and in 2003 was sworn in and assigned to the health committee. In those first years a bill came through the health committee dealing with asbestos. There are actually two major types of asbestos, one suspected of being much more dangerous than the other[2]. I proposed an amendment which simply gave CDPHE the prerogative to distinguish between the relative health risks of the two major types of asbestos. It was not a mandate, just statutory permission for the CDPHE to recognize the relative health risks between the two major types. It gave them the option of adjusting their regulations governing asbestos accordingly, if they considered it appropriate.

The committee saw the sense of it and passed the amendment. But when CDPHE found out, they used their power to kill the amendment when it got to the House floor. But why? It did not restrict them in any way. However, it was not something they had on their own agenda and they were used to having only their *own* agenda put into law, not something one of the people's representatives had produced.

This early experience with CDPHE taught me that they guard their power and control very carefully. It also taught me that they have a lot of power over the legislature, a lesson I was never to forget.

Following the asbestos issue through the years, I have had more than one constituent complain about the rigid and often illogical rules CDPHE has for asbestos abatement policies. I did what I could to help each of them work through this frustrating and expensive system, but it was never a good experience. CDPHE is bureaucratic, slow, expensive, and gives us some of the worst examples of why most citizens do not want to ever have to deal with government agencies.

Tented house for asbestos abatement

A few years ago the state association of asbestos abatement engineers asked me to speak at their annual meeting. I accepted, but warned them I would not hold back from my opinion that CDPHE was way over the top with asbestos regulations. Since asbestos abatement specialists benefit economically from these excessive regulations, I thought it wise to warn them I wanted to see a more straightforward way of dealing with asbestos problems.

With that caution in mind, they still said they wanted me and so I became their featured speaker for the event. After giving them my unvarnished opinion, I was surprised to find that about half of the room agreed with me. These professionals saw first-hand the devastation and horror stories of people who had their lives and property completely turned upside down by the CDPHE regulations. In the asbestos abatement industry, CDPHE has become more of a problem than a solution for the people of Colorado.

Diesel Emissions

While I was still in the Colorado House of Representatives, I learned much more about CDPHE from a single phone call. A gentleman, whom I had never met, called and said that since he had just retired from CDPHE he could finally call me without fear of losing his job. He told me he had worked in the diesel emissions inspection area of the department and went on to explain in detail how the diesel emissions program was an expensive and wasteful system which made virtually no difference in the quality of Colorado's air. About 99% of all vehicles passed inspection, and for those who did fail, the black smoke they emitted could be easily spotted by police in traffic and cited right then and there. Furthermore, the fees for a diesel emission inspection were very expensive; $50-$100. According to the caller, CDPHE kept the meaningless program because they collected a few bucks from every inspection and spent much of the money as if it were a slush fund for other projects.

It was obvious I needed to run a bill to reexamine this program and at least cut it back to a more reasonable level. Once again, CDPHE did not want to engage in an honest discussion on how to make this program better. They just wanted the bill killed, which they were very capable of accomplishing.

This experience, along with many other incidents, began to show me a clear pattern of how powerful and inflexible CDPHE had become.

Immunizations

Early in my legislative career I also discovered that CDPHE has a very heavy hand in overruling parental authority when it concerns vaccinations. They always claim they know better, despite the fact that thousands of highly educated parents have carefully studied this issue and have come to very different conclusions. The bottom line was always their road or no road.

In the early years, it was an incremental creep toward more and more control. They discounted all valid, documented concerns about the risks of vaccinations and tried to coerce parents to accept their ever-growing vaccination schedule, even for very small babies. When my son was born in 1984 there were only 7 vaccines required. Now there are at least 16, administered in more than 40 doses, and most of these are injected before the baby reaches two[3]. Any reasonable person can see that there should be an open, in-depth discussion about the number of vaccines, and the associated chemicals that we are injecting into young children. Vaccines are a major profit center for pharmaceutical companies, which in turn are heavy contributors to political campaigns.

There are still exemptions allowed from the vaccination mandate, but with the latest bill passed this year, (SB-163) parents will now have to endure multiple "reeducation" sessions (my words) to obtain a non-medical exemption. Additionally, the registration and tracking systems they have put in place include not just children. Most citizens in Colorado are now tracked in CDPHE's immunization-tracking database. Expect that tracking data to grow exponentially with COVID-19 vaccines just around the corner. Will they try to make that vaccine mandatory, without exemptions?

Let me take you back to 2015, when I was chairperson for the Senate health committee. Early in the session that year, CDPHE officials and lobbyists came to my office and said they had a great idea that would make immunization exemptions much simpler. Rather than having parents submit a written statement to their school's nurse, parents would be required to fill out a form online, directly with the department. I listened and tried to not sound too negative, but did warn them that a lot of parents consider a centralized registration system invasive and coercive. The officials and their lobbyists left my office, ignored my concerns, and promptly had their bill introduced in the House.

Hundreds of parents responded, opposing the legislation. They made thousands of phone calls and then attended committee meetings into the wee hours of the night. The hearings for this bill, and the bills they have introduced every year since then, have had more people show up to testify against than we had ever seen before in the legislature. In that first year, the bill died. But they proceeded to generate the online system anyway! Later, we found out it had been in the works months before the legislative session had even begun. They weren't looking for direction from the legislature. They just wanted a rubber stamp of approval for what they had already put in place.

Rally in Opposition to SB20-163

By the way, the online form they had prepared was so coercive that a national legal defense group prepared a federal lawsuit to fight the online form's language. The online form would have forced parents to make statements they knew to be untrue. Finally, just days before the suit was to be filed, the department relented and modified the form. But they continued to push their online registration system and had bills reintroduced until this year. This year, despite thousands of parents showing up in opposition, SB-163 passed, essentially on a party-line vote, and was signed by the governor. This bill gave them just about everything they wanted, including a requirement that forces parents to go through re-education training if they wish to deviate from the CDPHE immunization schedule.

One final note on immunizations. When I was on the Joint Budget Committee, I challenged the director of CDPHE, who assured me he knew all about the risks of vaccinations, to show me what he knew. After several weeks, his staff produced a couple of pages of what was a very shallow understanding of the documented risks of vaccinations. That demonstrated to me that even the director of CDPHE, who was a pediatrician, had almost no knowledge of the issue. He just knew the CDPHE party line.

I will stop here on the immunization issue, but a whole book could be written on this one aspect of government overreach here in Colorado.

Paint and Other Petroleum Products

If you buy a gallon of paint in Colorado, you will be charged a fee (think tax) to recycle surplus paint in the state. It doesn't matter if you will never need to recycle a drop of paint, you still must pay the fee, which adds up to several million dollars a year collected from the people of Colorado.

Additionally, as of May first of this year, oil-based paint and dozens of other useful petroleum based products have been outlawed in Colorado. You can thank CDPHE for these "enhancements" to our lives. Through regulations and their power over the legislature they have doubled down on making these useful, everyday products more expensive or even unavailable.

When I first learned of the oil paint ban I thought it was a false rumor, for there had been no legislation specifically authorizing such an extreme change in state policy. However, when I looked deeper, I found that CDPHE did this through rule-making alone. This time they didn't even try to get specific legislative authority to ban oil paint; they made up the law on their own!

This is one more example of how they abuse their authority and power to push their agenda of control over our everyday lives.

Life Issues and Sex Education

I have observed that a strong ally of CDPHE through the years has been Planned Parenthood. Whenever there is a push for radical changes to public school sex education policies, CDPHE is there urging adoption of the measure and Planned Parenthood is right there with them. Why would this be?

Follow the money. CDPHE controls a lot of money that eventually gets into the hands of Planned Parenthood. You won't find a line item in their budget for Planned Parenthood because it is more carefully hidden, but anytime the term "family planning "comes up, think Planned Parenthood. Every year CDPHE funnels funds to local county health departments and from there they are dispersed to "family planning" services.

The Colorado constitution prohibits all state funds from being used "directly or indirectly "for abortion (except to save the life of the mother), but ever since the people put that provision into the Colorado constitution in 1984, CDPHE has continued to find ways to keep revenue flowing to the major source of abortions in Colorado, Planned Parenthood.

The most dangerous attempt to fund Planned Parenthood came in 2020 in the form of SB-156, which would have required private insurance companies to pay all expenses related to "family planning" services, before any policy deductibles. This bill involved several state departments, and CDPHE was one of the players. Fortunately, the bill was finally killed at the end of this year's extraordinary session, a casualty of COVID-19. This bill, had it become law, would have guaranteed a permanent funding stream for the major abortion provider in the state. Expect to see the bill back in 2021.

Another controversial agenda that is common with CDPHE and Planned Parenthood is sex education. In 2019, one of the biggest bills was HB-1032, creating new standards for sex education. And if you dig a little deeper you find that Planned Parenthood is, you guessed it, the main provider of the curriculum for these sex education courses.

Emissions Standards

Anything that might be considered a threat to our environment comes under the umbrella of CDPHE regulations, such as regulations for vehicle emissions, oil and gas production, other industrial sources, and water standards.

Everyone wants clean air, uncontaminated water, and a healthy, nurturing environment, particularly here in colorful Colorado. But CDPHE takes this to the extreme, and what we end up with are ultra-expensive regulations for where we live, what we drive, when we drive, our energy costs, water usage, and waste systems. Some paints and other petroleum products have been banned, and the coal, oil, and gas industries are being intentionally regulated out of existence.

Now pollution is not just known toxic compounds, it also includes carbon dioxide, a common gas which is an essential part of the chemical cycle of life, and CDPHE has a whole new sandbox to play in. Chapter one and other chapters in this book covers much of the most recent legislation that enables CDPHE to develop significantly more intrusive regulations, which are designed to attempt to virtually eliminate human sources of carbon dioxide in Colorado.

With the laws this governor and his legislature have already created, CDPHE will have a much greater influence on our daily lives, and the cost of following their path will significantly diminish liberty and prosperity for all of the people of Colorado.

Infectious Diseases

The final area of CDPHE we will consider here is the actual area *usually* associated with public health; managing infectious diseases.

In 2020 this has been the dominant issue, as the Wuhan Virus has spread across the globe. In Colorado, CDPHE has been the driver of public information and public policy concerning the pandemic. This brings me back to where this chapter on CDPHE first began. The pandemic has tested the strengths and weaknesses of public health and we can see there are many changes that must be implemented to bring public health back to where it can be a benefit and a blessing to Colorado.

Earlier this year, 600 medical doctors sent a letter to the President saying that public health orders are actually jeopardizing the overall health of the public. [4] These MDs, from across the country and from many specialties, told the same story; public health orders intended to control the spread of COVID-19 are doing great damage to the physical and mental health of millions of Americans, eclipsing the dangers of COVID-19.

Most epidemiologists are sincerely trying to prevent disease, but the overall effect of public health has been a colossal failure. WHO, CDC, CDPHE, and local public health authorities have all contributed to this system that has been shown to be quite dysfunctional. Rather than objective and innovative scientists, who know how to quickly gather needed information and help policy makers develop effective plans of action, public health has become a bureaucratic system of outdated policies that give way too much power to unelected and *unaccountable* boards and directors.

Far too often their policies are driven by political decisions, rather than pure science. The World Health Organization continued to repeat reports from the Chinese government long after it was apparent the data was more propaganda than facts. The CDC took weeks to produce a valid test for the spread of COVID-19, burning up valuable time we needed to assess the situation. At the same time, they rejected systems already in place that could have given them a head start on determining where and when the disease was starting in our nation[5]. Treatment of the disease has also been fraught with a deep-state tone of approval and disapproval for different methods, based more on its political effect than its medical effect.

Quarantine seems to be the only plan they have. That may work when we catch a disease early, if it is localized or not very contagious, but to quarantine the entire state for months on end is causing far too many unintended consequences. One hard, cold truth that the health officials will not face is that a disease this contagious and this widespread cannot be quarantined away.

Initially, to "flatten the curve," there was some sense, when it looked like our medical systems could be overwhelmed like those in countries where their medical resources are not as robust as we enjoy. However, after the curve had become a flat, descending line, it was time to face the next step, which is get the country back to work as quickly as possible.

With a vaccine problematic and at least several months away, developing a herd immunity was and is the only real path out of this terrible situation. Those who consider themselves most vulnerable need to take all of the precautions they can, but the rest of the state should already have gone back to work, including doctors, who have patients with other ailments needing immediate attention.

One good thing we are finally figuring out, which public health should have been on top of months ago, is that the mortality rate for those who do contract COVID-19 is not much different than a bad flu strain. That means COVID-19 is a dangerous, highly contagious disease, but it is not magnitudes greater than what we deal with all the time. We can get through this, but only if we face the reality that most people who can get the disease will get the disease. Putting that herd-immunity off longer and longer will not make the problem go away, it just drags it out, making the other problems the shutdown creates even worse.

It is time for the elected leaders of our state to put public health back into their proper role. They must, once again, become objective scientists who are ready and able to give good counsel to our elected leaders and the public. Never again should public health become our unaccountable and unelected rulers.

Additionally, no Colorado governor should ever be allowed to abuse his/her emergency powers as Polis has for these many months.

I conclude with one straightforward solution that will help put CDPHE, local public health officials, and the governor back into their proper roles. It is a key component of our system of limited government called checks and balances.

- Require all extraordinary, emergency orders to get an official vote of approval from the appropriate group of elected officials for the order to continue.
    A. For county health departments this would mean approval from the county commissioners within five days.
    B. For CDPHE it should require the governor's explicit approval within five days, and the legislature's approval for any order that extends more than the original 30 days.
- All emergency orders from the governor should also be cancelled if he does not get specific legislative approval within 30 days. If they are not in session, in such a time of emergency they need to take the time to pass resolutions of approval. It can all happen in one legislative day.

Public health policy obviously has a vital role to play in today's complex society, but not with unilateral mandates from unelected and unaccountable bureaucrats. It is appropriate that they be expert advisers to elected officials, but they were never hired to be philosopher kings charged with micromanaging all of society.

The words of Thomas Jefferson still ring true: Governments are instituted among men to secure our unalienable rights of life, liberty and the pursuit of happiness. Public health policies must always remain consistent with that timeless principle, which applies to all of government, federal, state and local, without exception.

NOTES

1. Seaman, Jessica. *Colorado to declare racism a public health crisis after push by agency staffers to respond to protests, pandemic*, Denver Post, July 31, 2020.Denver Post.
https://www.denverpost.com/2020/07/31/colorado-racism-public-health-crisis/

2. Virta, Robert L. *Asbestos: Geology, Mineralogy, Mining, and Uses*, U. S. Department of Interior U. S. Geological Survey, Open File report 02-149.
https://pubs.usgs.gov/of/2002/of02-149/of02-149.pdf

3. Immunization Schedules. Centers for Disease Control and Previention
https://www.cdc.gov/vaccines/schedules/hcp/imz/child-adolescent.html

4. Turner, Grace-Marie. *600 Physicians Say Lockdowns Are A "Mass Casualty Incident"*, Forbes.com, May 22, 2020
https://www.forbes.com/sites/gracemarieturner/2020/05/22/600-physicians-say-lockdowns-are-a-mass-casualty-incident/#33f311d750fa

5. Fink, Sheri and Baker, Mike. New York Times. *'It's Just Everywhere Already': How Delays in testing set Back the U.S. Coronavirus Response.* March 10, 2020

https://www.nytimes.com/2020/03/10/us/coronavirus-testing-delays.html

7

THE PEOPLE'S HOUSE UNDER SIEGE: SMASHED WINDOWS, BROKEN PROMISES AND LOCK-STEP VOTING

BY DAVE WILLIAMS
Colorado State Representative

Ideas don't have consequences — only actions do. But bad ideas can lead to some of the most disastrous actions you can imagine. Colorado has not elected a Republican governor since 2002, and Democrats have dominated legislative elections over the same period. This dominance was achieved by a highly motivated and coordinated group of well-financed and politically smart individuals. This group didn't just talk about ideas, they got off the sidelines and made a difference because they were tired of seeing their side lose to Republicans cycle after cycle.

Before the 2004 election gave Colorado its first General Assembly in history with Democrat majorities in both chambers, Colorado Republicans had enjoyed electoral success for generations. This all came to a screeching halt when Democrats checked their personal egos at the door and decided that the different agendas from the various factions would all be better served if Democrats captured the majority.

Their unity efforts paid off, but the fruits of their labor wouldn't be fully understood until later. Not only did Democrats across the state gain power as never before, but they also opened the door to some of the most fringe elements of our society — to the point where, today, any moderation in their policy agenda has been thrown out the window.

The current crop of left-wing radicals who now control the policy agenda of the Colorado Democratic Party have shown their willingness to burn down the system and dismantle any traditional common ties that bind civil society together. In 2020, the public saw these radical Democrats march in the streets with rioters. These leftist militants, who currently find themselves as elected officials, are openly calling for "defunding" the police and the release of dangerous criminals back onto the streets, while also being fully supportive of the death penalty repeal and a stay of execution for several of the most heinous convicted murderers in Colorado's history.

These far-left politicians have now redefined the Democratic Party and will go on to redefine Colorado if left unchecked. This is readily apparent for anyone who watched the 2020 legislative session unfold during an unprecedented confluence of a public health epidemic, a declared state of emergency, an economic meltdown, and riots on Capitol grounds so violent and unpredictable that the Democratic leadership of the General Assembly decided to recess each day's business calendar before dark rather than risk the safety of the people's elected representatives.

From its start in early January, the legislative session normally ends the first week of May after 120 consecutive calendar days. But beginning on March 15, the Colorado General Assembly took a two-month hiatus that caused the session to extend to June 15. The last day of a 120-day session in 2020 normally would have been May 6, but as many Coloradans are now realizing, 2020 was anything but “normal.” (In fact, our Governor on April 26 signed an Executive Order establishing a "New Normal Advisory Board" of eleven appointed members. All eleven members are government officials and employees. Who better to "advise" the government than other government officials, right?)

What turned out to be a ten-week legislative recess was part of a public health strategy to slow the spread of the coronavirus, to "flatten the curve" of a global pandemic that wasn’t on many people’s radar a month earlier. When it became apparent that the Democrats' legislative agenda was threatened by a shorter session due to the long recess, they turned to the Colorado Supreme Court for help and political cover. The Democrats knew they couldn't just extend session on their own without major backlash from Republicans or the public in general.

To extend the session, Democrats needed to point to something as justification for violating the will of the voters and their oaths to the Colorado Constitution. They bet big on the one state government institution that had been filled with appointees (six out of the seven) who were mostly chosen by past Democratic governors. It would prove to be a smart move on their part. Democrats essentially asked permission to violate the Colorado Constitution by redefining what "120 calendar days" means.

Ask any normal person, or for a quicker response from your loan or credit lender, what the term "calendar days" means, and everyone outside of politics would agree that normally it is a substitute term for "consecutive days." But the year 2020 being officially NOT normal, the English language, too, had to be adjudicated.

The Democrats caught a break from the seven judges of the Colorado Supreme Court, who, in a close 4-3 decision, gave them the unprecedented power to redefine clear terms and pass laws outside of the timeframe established in the Colorado Constitution. According to the freshly sanctified "new normal," the 120-calendar day session could well run into July.

But even with this troubling court victory, the policy agenda the Democrats were trying to accomplish before the end of the session had to be retooled. It was universally accepted in the Capitol and elsewhere that political reality in Colorado had shifted as a result of the pandemic and social chaos caused by the economic shutdown ordered by Governor Polis' never-ending executive orders.

People started to feel the disruption and damage to our economy and healthcare system. As a result of a constant barrage of media coverage of rising COVID-19 cases, the perception among the public and legislators' constituents was that Coloradans were at risk of becoming ill or even dying, and those lucky enough to still have their health were at risk of either losing their jobs or being furloughed. Thus, the more moderate Democrats instinctively knew that in this atmosphere, pushing their ambitious, radical pre- COVID-19 policy agenda likely would turn off voters.

So, what was the Democrats' solution?

Most seasoned political operatives figured that Coloradans didn't care to support extreme policy goals – like radical Democrats' proposed prohibition of restaurants providing plastic straws to their customers – when the state was facing the most acute economic crisis in its history. So, Democratic leadership decided during the ten-week recess to make what they considered to be safe political promises, even over initial objections from many of their own members.

Democratic leadership announced their new, modified agenda broadly:

- Weeks before the 2020 session resumed on May 26, Democratic leadership committed to both the press and Republican leaders that controversial bills already introduced would be scrapped.
- They additionally proclaimed that any bills moving toward the Governor's desk would be mostly focused on coronavirus relief, as well as being "fast, friendly,

and free," meaning bills not needing additional government spending.

For a time, the Democrats did make reasonable efforts at stopping a portion of their agenda. They did follow through on killing a plan that would punish Christian healthcare sharing ministries like Medi-Share. They also ended their fight to pass more gun control measures like the so-called "safe storage" bill that would make it harder for gun owners to defend themselves, or the so-called "lost and stolen" bill that would potentially criminalize victims of stolen firearms and create a new gun owner registry.

Another example of Democrats trying to course correct came with a useless food labeling bill that encouraged food suppliers to do what they had already been doing. Everyone rightly understood that hard-working families cared more about making ends meet or paying the mortgage during a global crisis than worrying about their state representative passing a fluff environmental bill with no substance. It, too, quickly got the boot.

But like the scorpion in the story "The Scorpion and the Frog," the Democrats' nature would turn out to be self-destructive regardless of the promises they made. Anyone familiar with this fable understands that no matter how beneficial it was for the scorpion to not sting the frog in the back, the scorpion couldn't help himself, and, in the end, doomed them both.

So, soon after the session resumed at the end of May, Democrats made an about face and decided to not keep their word. In their minds, the voters gave them a mandate and they needed to plow ahead at all costs, pandemic or not, broken promises or not.

What hastened and partially rationalized their decision to break their commitment was the nearly $3-billion-dollar budget shortfall (for the combined current year budget and the fiscal year 2020-2021 budget). Democrats felt compelled to do something that would make John Maynard Keynes spin in his grave – cut the budget and lower government spending. However, reducing the budget was really a no-brainer, since, by law, Colorado had to adopt a balanced budget. So, with universal forecasts of severely reduced revenues over the coming two-year period, cuts to state spending were unavoidable.

The budget crisis produced much weeping and gnashing of teeth from all Democrats. For the rest of the session, the atmosphere was like a funeral. Democrats, who always bragged about "governing" didn't want any part of what would come next – facing the special interest groups that gave them their majorities and telling them they had no choice but to scale back their pet programs.

But Democrats weren't going down the road of responsible spending and austerity without a fight. They would once again embark on the quixotic task of trying to dismantle their much-hated Taxpayer Bill of Rights (universally known across Colorado as TABOR). The 4-2 Democrat majority on the powerful Joint Budget Committee (JBC) sprang into action. They would pursue measures that were aimed at "raising revenue" and start a messaging campaign to explain why they should not have to ask permission from voters before increasing taxes as TABOR requires.

Top Democrats in leadership would also seek to eliminate the Senior Homestead and Disabled Veteran Tax Exemption, an exemption worth a total of $164 million in lower taxes for eligible Coloradans, which allows certain seniors and veterans to avoid becoming homeless for failure to pay property taxes. Other Democrats would push for business tax hikes during an economic shutdown that saw an unprecedented increase in unemployment, and many of those businesses were closing for good. If there were a way to squeeze blood out of a turnip, the Democrats were determined to find it.

This "go-for-it" attitude wasn't confined to only the state budget. Democrats pushed forward legislation that forced all employers in Colorado to provide up to six days of paid medical leave to their employees. Needless to say, businesses will do one of three things in response to higher costs imposed by government: they'll hire fewer workers, cut work hours for existing employees, or they'll go bankrupt. These realities led to strong opposition from the business community and any reminders about promises of "fast, friendly, and free" legislation fell on deaf ears.

A bill that allows state workers to unionize and collectively bargain against taxpayers was muscled across the finish line by Joint Budget Committee Chair, Rep. Daneya Esgar. This new law will not only increase costs to taxpayers by untold millions, but it will also create a new source of campaign money for Democrats. That money will be collected through member dues and funneled through the union that helped advocate for the bill's passage.

Rep. Kyle Mullica finally saw his pet issue adopted with the passage of SB20-163, the "School Entry Immunization Act." This bill had extreme and fierce opposition from citizens of all partisan backgrounds who opposed eroding parental rights, limiting Colorado immunization exemptions, and promoting further profits for pharmaceutical companies who manufacture and sell vaccines. This was one of the few bills of the extended session that drew big crowds to the Capitol despite a global pandemic. In fact, a very unusual Sunday noon hour committee hearing drew over one thousand citizens to protest the bill.

But of all the radical legislation the Democratic majority set out to pass despite their promises, those bills would pale in comparison to what they were able to ultimately pull off. In less than ten days, Democrats would rush through a so-called "police reform" bill, SB20-217, which was promoted and justified as a needed response to a police brutality incident in Minneapolis, where a black man, George Floyd, died while in police custody. A viral video of the ugly incident had been viewed by millions, resulting in protests and riots in many cities across the nation.

SB20-217 would be the capstone of the year's legislative session: something big enough to salvage what Democrats considered to be a disappointing session overall. But what happened next is truly shocking.

Like many other Denver nights, Thursday, May 28, was warm and beautiful with no storm clouds in sight. On this third day of the reconvened session, many legislators were in a hurry to wrap up a long day so we could enjoy the rest of the night with our families. Many, if not all of us, were finalizing our budget amendments that needed to be submitted ahead of the budget debate the following day. What made this year's budget amendment deadline more challenging than years prior was the shortened timeframe we were all working under. Democrats only gave us less than a week to study, debate, and amend a $30-billion-dollar state budget.

Many of us were looking forward to finishing our work and enjoying what would be a pleasant enough evening – or so we thought. Before the day's end, however, all legislators were notified about a recently scheduled protest against police brutality that was organized by local Black Lives Matter groups in the wake of the George Floyd death in Minneapolis earlier in the week.

Not a single legislator was too concerned about the planned protest in nearby Civic Center Park, which is two short blocks west of the Capitol. House legislative leadership had decided to make lawmakers work through the whole weekend to pass the budget bill, HB20-1360. After all, the Capitol had seen its fair share of peaceful protests involving thousands of people. Why would this one be any different?

Protesters had gathered on the west side of the Capitol by the time most lawmakers had left for the day. Some Democratic legislators had stayed to participate in the protests though. This was, of course, an opportunity for Democrats to be seen and play to their base. Representatives Leslie Herod and Jonathan Singer were both visibly present at the start of the protest rally; the goal for them was simple: show their solidarity for the cause and turn it into an opportunity to expand support for their personal brands. Did they care about the issue? Sure, but these are also politicians who search for ways to increase their public profile.

And they didn't let the occasion go to waste. Even in the midst of an unruly crowd, these Democrats wanted the protestors to know that they were on their side... at least until the gunshots were fired.

Someone in the crowd across the street at Civic Center Park had fired gunshots at state patrol officers near the west steps of the Capitol. Immediately after the shooting, lawmakers and Capitol employees were told by Colorado State Patrol emergency text messages to shelter-in-place inside the Capitol complex. Meanwhile, many of the so-called protestors outside became increasing violent, and the protest itself quickly turned into a full-fledged riot.

As the sun was setting, rioters openly associated with Antifa and BLM started destroying public and private property while encouraging others to do the same. The State Capitol, along with the many monuments and government buildings surrounding it, were vandalized and defaced. Windows were smashed and radical, pornographic graffiti was going up everywhere within reach.

At one point, a large mob tried storming the Capitol to breach the locked doors. Not many people were aware of this at the time, but State Patrol was in full riot gear reinforcing the barricades and preparing for a possible breach. While the mob was trying to knock down the doors, they were chanting “Black Lives Matter!” and tagging the Capitol's outer stone walls with phrases like “Fuck the Police,” “All Cops Are Bastards,” “Fuck White People,” “Eat the Rich,” “Death to the Man in Blue,” and drawing numerous images of the communist hammer and sickle.

During every session, lawmakers routinely park their vehicles in "the circle" parking lot surrounding the Capitol on all sides. In a moment of cruel irony for Democratic Senate President Leroy Garcia, the rioters converged on his black GMC pick-up truck and started to destroy it. Matt Mauro, a reporter with KDVR FOX31, posted a video of President Garcia’s truck being attacked. His truck was heavily damaged with all tires being slashed and every window being smashed. It was later reported that President Garcia was eventually evacuated out of the Capitol via the old tunnel system underneath the complex. The rioters would also go on to destroy several State Patrol vehicles that night.

But it didn't end there. The riot continued past midnight. The rioters even split into separate groups with many of them walking to I-25, blocking the highway and causing major traffic congestion. Others decided to destroy or deface property near the downtown area and the 16th Street Mall. Police were attacked with projectiles that included water bottles, rocks, or anything that could be thrown that would cause harm.

The chaos around the State Capitol complex caused leadership to quickly postpone the legislative work that was still pending for the next several days. The Democrats, trying to put the best spin on the situation, said they were delaying work so that they could give the so-called protestors "space" and express their "solidarity" for the cause of police reform.

Senate President Garcia was even gracious in response to his truck being destroyed. The Pueblo Chieftain reported Garcia as saying *"Material things can be replaced . . . We have a lot of work to do to repair and ensure the trust is there for the general public, and I share in that responsibility as an elected official in the state of Colorado and I am going to be making sure in the coming weeks that we are having these types of conversations."*

The fix was in for Colorado law enforcement as well. If the Democratic Senate President wasn't going to condemn the rioters after they destroyed his own personal property, then what hope would there be for any sensible, balanced policy discussion aimed at "police reform?" The rioters had just proved that they could create havoc, suffer no consequences, and force Democratic lawmakers to move in the policy direction they demanded.

As a result, and to no one's surprise, the riots continued for several nights. Public and private property kept being destroyed and defaced. More rioters showed up to later demonstrations than in prior nights. Denver police and the State Patrol were outnumbered and having a tough time dealing with the rioters to the point that many of them were working off few to no hours of sleep. And the Mayor of Denver, Michael Hancock, was painfully slow to act in the face of buildings being damaged and defaced, Molotov cocktails being thrown, cops getting hurt, and statues being torn down. Governor Polis was also invisible and silent that first week of violence.

Both the Mayor and Governor would eventually issue weak statements calling for peace. More than a week after the riots began, Mayor Hancock would issue a citywide curfew order only after public outcry became too much for him to ignore – an order very loosely enforced.

At no point did Democrats in power ever denounce the rioters. Instead several lawmakers excused away their criminal behavior. In fact, on the following Sunday after three straight nights of rioting, Rep. Leslie Herod appeared on the George Brauchler Radio Show and told listeners that she didn't want to see any rioters behind bars because *"the damages would be recouped by the private insurance companies anyways."*

So, instead of denouncing these criminals and restoring public safety, the Democrats were busy drafting a sweeping anti-police bill, and Rep. Herod was determined to lead the charge as a member of the Black Democratic Legislative

Caucus. While most were distracted by the carnage of the riots, Rep. Herod, along with the ACLU and several other Democratic lawmakers, were negotiating the details of their far-reaching anti-police bill without the input of Republicans or members of the law enforcement community.

Unbeknownst to many of us, Rep. Herod was even excused from debating and voting on amendments during the most consequential budget debate in Colorado's history so she could address a Black Lives Matter protest on the progress of her anti-police bill.

Rep. Herod's initial draft of her police reform bill was so outrageous that it made many other Democrats blush. For instance, Rep. Herod wanted to create a new gun registry for gun owners involved in any traffic stops. Why is that information needed in order to eliminate police brutality? Simply put, it's not. It was thrown in there because of Rep. Herod's extreme anti-gun beliefs.

Another example of how extreme Herod's early draft was can be seen in a section allowing criminals who committed certain felonies to not be initially arrested. She wanted to force district attorneys to commit to prosecution ahead of time before any arrests were made. In other words, she wanted to stop police from making arrests on the spot when they witnessed a felony in real-time, which would allow criminals to be a greater flight risk: they wouldn't ever have to face a judge or jury.

Rep. Herod had to be talked off the ledge, and it came to the point where Senate Democrats stepped in and decided to tone it down by starting the bill in their chamber where it could be more reasonably managed and amended.

Senate Republicans, along with the law enforcement lobby,

had two paths from which to choose. They could outright oppose any bill introduced, and likely lose that battle given the atmosphere, or they could try to improve the bill by amendments to the point where they could promise their support.

Either choice was tough, they were certainly between a rock and a hard place. All Republicans agreed that we needed to make reforms to policing, especially in light of the George Floyd incident, but what the Democrats proposed was way beyond what was necessary or desirable. So, with a figurative gun pointed at their heads, Senate Republicans decided to make an atrocious bill tolerable with the expectation that it would pass in a bi-partisan fashion. Senate Republicans worked with law enforcement to craft amendments that would mitigate the likely damage. Their working theory was that Democrats wanted a public relations victory more than a pure policy win. Democrats definitely had the numbers to pass whatever they wanted, but they also didn't want a long drawn out fight in the middle of riots that were also happening in a global pandemic.

Democrats wanted to be seen as responsive in the wake of George Floyd's death, so they could bolster their brand in the area of criminal justice reform. They also figured that this was a no-win scenario for Republicans. Republicans would either be forced to agree with Democrats on this issue or fight against it at the risk of being seen as supportive of corrupt cops. In the minds of Senate Republicans, the only reasonable move that allowed for greater balance in the bill was for them to pledge their votes if certain amendments from law enforcement were adopted.

After the bill was heavily amended and sent to the House Chamber, Rep. Herod threatened that any amendments adopted that weren't previously approved by her would cause the bill to revert to its originally introduced version. She wasn't going to tolerate anything that would jeopardize her efforts. Many of us in the House rightfully accused her of extortion but in the end, what choice did House Republicans have?

After the dust settled, all but two Senate Republicans voted to support the amended bill, and in the House, eleven out of twenty-four Republicans joined them in voting for SB20-217.

It's hard to call this a victory. In my opinion, a more apt term for what was achieved by the Senate Republicans would be "successful failure." They did make a bad bill substantially better. The damage was mitigated, but would that bring any comfort to good cops who were now at risk of being punished for merely enforcing laws in good faith? Even though the bill was improved significantly, it still made it harder for the police to actually do a job that most politicians would never sign up for.

After hearing from rank and file cops, and their spouses, it was clear that police officers felt their jobs would become more difficult and dangerous. It was obvious that one of two things would occur as a result of this bill's passage: cops would be more risk averse to the point that arrests would decrease, or many would quit or not join the law enforcement profession at all.

It's important to note that the Colorado State Trooper responsible for leading the defense of the Capitol during the riots has taken another law enforcement job outside of Colorado. The unofficial reason for his departure was that his job became untenable with the passage of this anti-police legislation.

What transpired in 2020 under the Gold Dome may seem shocking at first glance, but it's not surprising to anyone who's been paying attention to Colorado politics for the past twenty years. This is the natural progression stemming from the takeover of Colorado by Democrats as outlined by Adam Schrager and Rob Witwer in the 2010 book, *"The Blueprint: How the Democrats Won Colorado and Why Republicans Everywhere Should Care."*

Colorado's "Gang of Four," which included Jared Polis, Tim Gill, Pat Stryker, and Rutt Bridges, spent millions of dollars to buy political power so they could bring to life their radical vision for our state. Their efforts, which started in 2002 but have continued on through today, have brought us to where we are now. Unfortunately, there are no clear signs that we will be getting off these progressives' destructive path anytime soon.

For years these wealthy "progressives" have spearheaded the funding of Colorado's demise. They built campaign infrastructures, funded leftist "non-profit advocacy" groups, recruited and trained candidates, helped create new election laws to further tip the scales, gerrymandered legislative districts for competitive advantage, funneled taxpayer dollars to their allies, and managed to deceive voters into electing Democratic candidates who are most often marketed as "moderates."

Amazingly, Democrats in the legislature now openly brag about how they campaign as "moderates" to get elected and then govern as far left as possible after they're sworn-in. Whether elected from districts in Durango, Pueblo, Ft. Collins or Thornton, east or west of the I-25 corridor, they vote 98% of the time the same as Boulder liberals – and laugh all the way to the proverbial bank.

From time to time, some Democratic lawmakers will attempt to split off and oppose certain left-wing policies, but it usually ends in severe punishment. In fact, it's commonplace for the Democratic Speaker of the House to leave the voting machine open longer than normal if not enough Democrats vote "correctly." In this scenario, Democratic leadership will apply pressure in real-time to force someone's vote to flip. There have even been instances where other Democrats will physically surround one of their own on the House floor and not-so-subtly pressure that member into changing their position.

Additionally, Democrats are discouraged from having any independent thought by being threatened with a primary election challenge from one of the hundreds of potential candidates the left's political machine is constantly grooming. It is widely believed that Democratic leadership also has "dossiers" of politically damaging information on all their elected officials as insurance against anyone who steps too far out of line.

Traditional Republican leaders – who are euphemistically called the "Republican Establishment" – also share in the blame for where Colorado government is now. They enjoyed legislative majorities for decades and didn't do much to block a hostile takeover. For two decades now, Republican leaders have failed to adapt to the new rules of the game as practiced by Democrats, rules many people have come to learn from *Alinsky's Rules for Radicals*. They constantly keep fighting political battles with the obsolete and ineffective tools and tactics of the past.

Many Republicans refuse to get "ugly" while not realizing they are already in the middle of a gutter fight, which by definition is "ugly." The "Gang of Four" changed how

Democrats fight political battles, while Republicans worry about funding for one more poll or what the press may say about them. Thus, too many Republicans help the left's censorship by censoring themselves.

Today, the Republican Party is not as united as it must be to survive. Too many moderate Republicans prioritize displacing conservative candidates, who truly believe in the Republican principles, over defeating Democrats in the general election. Sadly, there are even some influential Republicans who have given up the fight for a Republican majority and are resigned to the inevitability of socialist hegemony.

So, where does the "Party of Lincoln" go from here? If we want to start winning and turning Colorado around, then Colorado Republicans need to chart a different path.

First, we need to accept that Democrats won't give up power without a fight. The days of running a rosy, rainbows-and-butterflies campaign are over. To win, we need to consistently throw effective punches at our opponents that highlight how radical, out-of-touch, and morally bankrupt they are.

Regardless of how you feel about President Donald Trump, he proved that you can be a fighter and win. This is the winning attitude all Republicans need to adopt.

The truth is that most citizens don't trust either major political party, and the proof of that is in the ever-increasing voter registration of "unaffiliated voters" in our state. The people have a deep distrust of most politicians and think that they are corrupt on some level. People are hungry for leaders who will fight for them against a system that they believe sells them out year after year. The people deserve nothing less than a commitment from Republicans that we will *always* fight for them, for their rights, their jobs, their families, their safety, and their country.

Second, we need to stop eating our own. Republican leaders in every corner of the GOP need to adopt and follow the "big tent" model of political coalition-building. We all need to recognize and practice the axiom that success in politics is a matter of addition, not subtraction.

After the disastrous, Democrat-run 2020 session, winning back the majority should be much easier because the Democratic party is now openly and undeniably in the hands of radicals who will sacrifice even law enforcement and public safety to appease their extremist allies. It makes no difference whether a Democrat is elected from the mountain west or eastern plains, rural Larimer County or suburban Jefferson County, when they enter the legislative chamber to cast votes on hundreds of bills, they vote 98% of the time the same as Boulder liberals.

Third, any Republican who wants to lead needs to believe we can win majorities again and start building social, cultural and political infrastructure to that end. The Democrats have spent two decades creating and financing organizations outside of the formal party apparatus (which can legally avoid cumbersome campaign laws) that are mainly designed to give Democrats an electoral advantage. While partnering with wealthy center-right donors as well as grassroots organizations, we can create entities that will inspire citizens of all ages, races, ethnicities and religions to support Republican principles and candidates.

Anything short of that will allow radical Democrats to not only hold onto their majorities in both chambers but possibly achieve California-style supermajorities. Fortunately, in the centennial state there are enough Coloradans who still love America too much to let that happen. Yet, our good ideas won't change a thing unless we start giving priority to offense over defense and begin doing what is necessary to win back voters who already know the Democrats have left them behind

8

TYRANNY UNLEASED BY SINGLE PARTY CONTROL

BY ROB WOODWARD
Colorado State Senator

Throughout most of human history, humankind has been ruled by kings, queens, lords or brutal dictators. Then, nearly 250 years ago, a few brave men and women turned the world on its head by claiming that human rights are not dependent on rulers, but instead are bestowed by our Creator.

The founders of the United States established a written Constitution, codifying that the government's just powers are derived from the People, that laws are enacted through democratically elected representatives, and, ultimately, that those elected officials must act and govern according to the Rule of Law. The Constitution and regular, periodic elections help guarantee that the majority cannot easily abuse their power over the minority.

Tragically, in Colorado, we've witnessed a return to the days of tyrannical rule of the majority over the minority.

In 2019 and 2020, it became clear that Democratic Governor Jared Polis, the Democratic House Majority and the Democratic Senate Majority were going to take full advantage of the opportunity to push the Progressive agenda of radical legislation. This new "trifecta" dominated by Boulder Democrats held all the power of the state. Their agenda-driven legislation sped through the legislature and became law at lightning speed, hardly registering the concerns of thousands of Coloradans who voiced opposition.

Then at the start of the COVID-19 pandemic, the Governor seized new executive powers by signing an Emergency Declaration, allowing him to ignore, suspend or override certain existing laws, create new administrative rules, and spend billions of dollars on his own, without the input of the People's representatives in the legislative branch. He so enjoyed his new power that he repeatedly renewed his 30-day Declaration month after month after month — renewed six times from April to August. He effectively neutered the General Assembly and made it irrelevant.

The 2019 Democrat-controlled legislature led the nation in the embrace of the "Green New Deal." The primary battle that year centered around oil and gas; having just lost a statewide vote to establish extreme setback distances for oil and gas wells and infrastructure that would have essentially ended all petroleum development, the Governor and legislative Democrats decided to push Senate Bill 19-181, a regulatory nightmare that hung a bureaucratic millstone around the neck of an industry already struggling under a mass of mostly superfluous red tape.

During the intense debates over SB19-181, thousands of oil and gas workers, business owners and their families showed up on the Capitol steps and in committee hearings week after week to oppose this statutory assault on their livelihood. Farmers and ranchers explained desperately how the loss of mineral income would decimate agriculture. Economists made it clear that eliminating drilling would result in a dramatic reduction in state and local income taxes, revenue needed to fund our roads, schools, and emergency services. Energy producers testified that the forced, rapid conversion to "green energy" would egregiously increase the cost of electricity, and thus chase away manufacturing jobs.

The disciples of the Green New Deal agenda also pushed bills that subsidized wealthy Tesla drivers — by diverting state funds to tax credits for the purchase of these expensive electric cars, mandating utilities install charging stations, and by shifting the energy costs onto the backs of the seniors, who would be forced to pay for these subsidies through higher utility bills. The AARP came out strongly against this and other related Democrat social engineering efforts, but their concerns, too, were ignored.

In 2019 the "big ask" by the Governor was all-day

kindergarten. He made it clear that we MUST include that in the budget. At a time when teachers and school districts were begging for more state funding, the state legislature expanded the schools' obligation to teach more kids using a low-ball amount of seed money to get it started. The Democrat trifecta refused to listen to alternatives, such as a proposal that would send more money to districts but let them choose whether to launch all-day Kindergarten or fill some other holes in their local budgets. Since this new unfunded mandate on local school districts was based on lowball cost estimates, teacher salaries were in peril even before the COVID-19 pandemic led the Democrat Governor to shut down the state's economy.

The other notable legislation pushed in 2019 was the war on small business. Well-meaning legislators invented all kinds of ways to ostensibly help employees, even though the cost to the employers was prohibitive and untenable. The opposition from small business owners was overwhelming, and also loud enough to forestall some of the worst proposals. Nevertheless, most of the punitive legislation became law.

By the end of my first year in the Senate, I realized that our committee "hearings" were mostly a sham. There was no listening to public testimony. I saw testimony cut short. I saw the Democratic committee chairs yell, swear, and cut off Senators who were asking difficult questions. I saw clear and compelling evidence routinely ignored. The Democrat majority legislators were clearly NOT hearing the testimony; they were simply going through the motions. Most hearings were deeply disappointing and troubling.

The Republicans in the Senate finally slowed down the train by flexing constitutional muscles against the Senate

Leadership by exercising the right to have bills read at length before a final vote. It took a Supreme Court ruling to enforce our rights, but even that valiant effort was but a speed bump. After that legal victory, the velocity at which bad legislation was being churned out of the Majority office onto the Governor's desk was slowed, but too much still became law.

The summer and fall of 2019 were chock-full of legislative work. Although the people of Colorado had voted to limit the legislative work of their citizen legislature to 120 days each year, the Democrats decided they wanted to hold hearings and draft bills during the other eight months, too. It was no wonder that 2020 was a record-breaking year of hundreds of pieces of new legislation.

The 2020 session got off to a very odd start: we spent the first two months talking about mostly unsubstantial legislation. We debated bills about circus animals, argued whether it was appropriate for legislators to insert the names of their dogs into bills, and changed the name and date of a state holiday. We invented new government programs and searched for ways to circumvent the Taxpayer Bill of Rights.

By mid-March the pandemic fears struck Colorado, with the first COVID-19 death reported on March 4 and Governor Polis signing a Declaration of public health emergency on March 11. The Legislature soon went into a formal recess for two weeks.

The Senate made a one-day return to the Capitol on the appointed date. Republicans showed up, but most Democrats stayed home. What happened next was nothing less than bizarre. The Senate's Democrat President, Leroy Garcia, ordered the Colorado State Patrol to lock the doors to the Senate Chambers and *specifically ordered them not to allow any Senator to enter the chambers*. This had never been done before. I believe that the Democrats realized that the minority Republicans had the legal authority under Senate rules to call the Senate to order each morning. Although we were unlikely to have achieved a quorum, it would have allowed Republicans to call attention to the fact that the Governor had appropriated all legislative powers to himself.

I showed up to work morning after morning, hoping that I could regain access to my desk on the Senate floor. I figured, since we were getting paid, we should probably go to work. The state's new ruling class thought differently.

Eventually, the Democrats decided on a date to reconvene, the Tuesday after Memorial Day. Conveniently, that gave the Governor the ability to disburse billions of dollars of money from the Federal CARES Act the week before, because he just couldn't — or wouldn't — wait for the normal budget process.

We were told by the Majority leadership that upon reconvening, legislators could suggest new legislation only if it was "Fast, Friendly, and Free" – meaning bills that were uncontroversial, bipartisan, and which bore no fiscal impact. Republicans were pleasantly surprised, but quite happy, that we would be focused solely on emergency bipartisan measures that were needed at that unique moment in history. We were going to limit new legislation to responding to the urgent needs of the moment, and to bring some relief to folks who were suffering from the economic shutdown.

Of course, before long, the bipartisanship ended. The Democrats soon reverted to their ideological program of reordering society, and began proposing legislation that was both expensive and unflinchingly hostile to economic recovery, particularly to small business.

Normally, the Capitol is buzzing with energy as lobbyists and the public show up to committee hearings. But a media blitz convinced the public that we preferred that they not come to the Capitol because of the risk of spreading the COVID-19 infection. Then, at the end of the first week of the renewed session, as anti-police protests turned violent, the public became even more afraid of coming to the Capitol. During June, we sat in hearings where at times the entire room was empty. As there was no public testimony to challenge the Progressive agenda, it sailed through the process over Republican dissent. And because the Governor, the Denver Mayor and the Denver DA were powerless — or unwilling — to protect us, all legislative business was concluded before dark. Absent any confidence that Denver Police would protect us, we had to escape the building each day before the rioters could attack.

Admittedly, a natural part of my frustration, then as now, was in seeing so many left-wing Progressive policies with which I disagreed enacted into law. To a certain extent, that fact shows how well our American political system works: elections have consequences. In November of 2018, the voters of Colorado elected Democrats into the majority in both the House and the Senate and the Governor's Office. That gave them the power to write bills and enact laws without a single Republican vote — and they are doing that, to the celebration of the state's major media and the interest groups that finance their campaigns.

Yes, our democratic form of government gives Democrats and Republicans the right to pursue their policy agenda when they win majorities in the legislature — even if the agenda is more radical than the platform they campaigned on. However, something new and deeply worrisome has been added to the mix since November of 2018.

What *was* objectionable, what was new in 2019 and 2020, was the radical, absolutist approach, and the persistent disregard for any structural or inherent check on their power. Constitutional restraints were dismissed out of hand. They were too often unwilling to listen to criticism about their bills. They pushed too fast and too hard in their overreach, without any consideration of real-world consequences.

What is new and worrisome in the passion and intensity displayed by the Democrat Majority during much of the 2020 session is the evident goal of enacting changes that will be systemic and irreversible should Republicans ever retake the majority. Democrats appear ready to make changes that in fact alter the constitutional and institutional protections embodied in our state constitution, the federal Bill of Rights, and the God-given rights which Jefferson summarized in the phrase, "Life, liberty and the pursuit of happiness."

What the Democrats displayed in the 2019 and 2020 sessions was not a love of governance but the love of power. We have seen that in other times and other countries, and folks, it usually does not end well. What we saw in the 2020 session was not activist governance; this was ideological fervor that sought an end regardless of the means or the costs. The economic and social damage from these recklessly pursued policies are just starting to be felt.

Unfortunately, this damage will compound the harm inflicted from the economic shutdown ordered by our multimillionaire Governor, Jared Polis. The state budget will be dismal in the coming two or three years, likely saved from the fiscal abyss only by TABOR, our flat rate income tax, and our state constitution's balanced budget requirement.

The most obvious symbol of Democratic failure is the condition of Capitol Building itself. In an effort to satisfy the demands of their most ideologically zealous supporters, the Governor's minions ordered the Colorado State Patrol to stand down, allowing protestors — armed with bricks, baseball bats and paint spray cans — to attack our State Capitol night after night for more than two months. Meanwhile, Democratic leadership in the House and Senate oddly missed numerous opportunities to condemn the violence.

Coloradans are beginning to wake up to the dangers of tyrannical single party control and the damage that can result, especially when the political party in power is dismissive of conventional standards and respect for public safety, property rights and law and order. Until Colorado voters act to restore a balance of power at the Capitol, it is likely that the radical Boulder trifecta will continue to vandalize our state.

9

DEMOCRATS' 2020 TAX REFORM BILL: KICKING THE ECONOMY TO THE CURB

BY PATRICIA KURGAN
Political Analyst

The Colorado business community entered the 2020 session of the Colorado General Assembly with considerable skepticism, not knowing if Democrats would continue their all-out assault on businesses as happened in the 2019 session or pursue a more cautious agenda — as is customary when members are facing reelection in November. The answer was quick in coming. Business was on the defense again as job killing measures were introduced daily in the first weeks of the session.

The arrival of the COVID-19 pandemic in early March brought everything to a halt and a reappraisal. After Governor Polis' March 11 Declaration of a public health emergency, the legislature went into recess and did not reconvene for legislative business until ten weeks later.

Conversations with the Democrat majority's leaders around

the Capitol during the long recess indicated that many of the controversial business-related bills would be left for the next session. That plan was shared with Republican leaders as well. Everyone expected Priority One would be given to the state budget as a 2-year combined deficit of over $3 billion (in the current FY2020 and coming year FY2021 budgets) needed to be addressed, hopefully in a largely bipartisan manner. Next in importance was the School Finance Act, which always follows the adoption of the annual budget, and finally about two dozen “Sunset” bills reauthorizing various professional licensing rules and regulations which would automatically expire July 15 without that reauthorization.

This setting aside of all other legislation in the extended session was not just because everyone wanted to get along in tough times. Any other legislation would be in violation of the rule that allowed the legislature to meet after an extended recess, House and Senate Joint Rule 44. It allows a suspension of the constitutionally limited 120 calendar day session (which the Colorado Supreme Court upheld by a bare majority 4-3 decision) but requires that only “mission critical” legislation be considered after the session is allowed to extend beyond the 120 calendar day limit.

That was the expected plan when the legislators reconvened on May 26, but Democrats instantly showed they had no intention of keeping their word by honoring that plan. Their radicalism glowed in their eagerness to move their policy agenda to enactment as quickly as possible. The compressed session calendar on May 26 forced the majority to kill a few less-important "message bills" in committee, but contrary to the plan announced during the recess, began introducing many new bills quite radical in their scope and fiscal impact. In the Senate twenty new bills were introduced after the session resumed in May, and in the House, besides the state budget and necessary budget-related "orbital bills," 26 new bills were launched.

Living in their government bubble, Democrats showed their ignorance of the financial ruin that everyday people were experiencing as a direct result of the Governor's unilateral shutdown orders. No state government workers lost their jobs under those orders, but Colorado's unemployment had jumped from 2.7% in February to over 14% in April. State Government was full of foreboding because of the budget outlook, but in May and June, all the pain and sacrifice was happening in the private sector, especially in small businesses.

New bills were introduced that would immediately impact employers' bottom lines, and thus, their employees as well. Tens of thousands of business owners were perplexed: they were fighting literally for their survival, and yet, legislators were busy adding more taxes, fees and regulations which would only add to their burdens and lessen their chances of survival. Business owners lucky enough to still be open scrambled to pay rent, utilities and their employees' payroll and benefits. People who were no longer employed questioned if and when they could go back to work, and how they would provide for their families. In that environment, small businesses were suffering the most. According to a 2018 Small Business report there were 611,495 small businesses in Colorado, or 99.5% of all Colorado businesses as defined in Colorado law. More to the point, small businesses employed 1.1 million people, 48.6% of the state workforce.[1]

The most egregious bill came with only days remaining before the end of the session. On June 8, seven days before adjournment, the *Tax Expenditure Adjustment Act,* HB 20-

1420[2], was introduced with four Democrat sponsors. That was the formal title of the bill, but Democrats widely referred to it as the "Tax Fairness Bill." After all, it was only "fair" that Colorado businesses not get tax deductions connected to the Trump Administration's 2017 tax reform bill. That was an article of faith among progressives, regardless of the popularity and value of the federal tax reform all across the Colorado business community.

HB20-1420

BY REPRESENTATIVE(S) Sirota and Gray, Benavidez, Gonzales-Gutierrez, Jaquez Lewis, Kipp, Lontine, Weissman, Woodrow, Arndt, Bird, Buckner, Buentello, Caraveo, Cutter, Duran, Esgar, Herod, Hooton, Jackson, Kennedy, Kraft-Tharp, McCluskie, Michaelson Jenet, Mullica, Singer, Snyder, Tipper, Valdez A., Valdez D.;
also SENATOR(S) Moreno and Hansen, Bridges, Danielson, Fenberg, Fields, Foote, Ginal, Gonzales, Pettersen, Story, Todd, Williams A., Winter, Garcia.

CONCERNING THE ADJUSTMENT OF CERTAIN STATE TAX EXPENDITURES IN ORDER TO ALLOCATE ADDITIONAL REVENUES TO THE STATE EDUCATION FUND, AND, IN CONNECTION THEREWITH, MAKING AN APPROPRIATION.

On the last day of the session, June 15, a heavily amended version of HB20-1420 was passed by the Senate and then immediately re-passed by the Democrat majority in the House, with no Republican votes supporting it. A few days later it was signed by the Governor.

To say the least, this was a very fast-tracked bill and added to the confusion for those working to follow it through the legislative process. The business community was never asked for input as the bill was being drafted. In fact, business leaders had been assured privately beginning in March that such legislation would not be pursued in 2020. Yet, the majority Democrats again broke their word and pursued a different strategy: hit hard and fast, take advantage of the disruptions (protest rallies and riots), avoid confrontation, deflect any criticism regarding earlier statements, pass the bill and then get out of town.

Restrictions on entry into the Capitol and potential threats to personal safety were present due to protests and riots. Testimony on the bill from business organizations in committees was limited. Substantial amendments were presented during committee hearings and voted on immediately. Audio of testimony was not available after committee hearings, which immensely limited understanding of the bill by interested parties who could not attend the hearings in person. Committee hearing notes were not always posted. Debates on the House and Senate floors were perfunctory. Transparency was replaced with speed. This bill had to pass, and pass quickly without any interference.

The business community stood in unity questioning "Why now?" stunned that excessive taxation on businesses was even under consideration. Democrat legislators passed the bill (not one Republican supported it) believing that additional revenue would be generated in order to back fill state revenue gaps, specifically to "allocate additional revenues to the State Education Fund. In other words, "for the children".

Although it has nothing to do with education, there is also a provision in the bill that expands the EITC, Earned-Income Tax Credit, a tax break for low-income workers. The requirement for a social security number in order to receive the tax credit has been repealed, allowing residents, regardless if they are in the United States legally or illegally, to claim this benefit on their Colorado tax return.

In essence, this bill stripped deductions that businesses were granted by the federal bi-partisan bill passed by Congress in late March, *Coronavirus Aid Relief and Economic Security Act,*[3] also known as the CARES Act. Acknowledging that government itself is responsible for millions of business closures — something that the Democrat-dominated Colorado state legislature has NOT yet acknowledged— the federal government concluded that financial aid needed to be quickly distributed to businesses and working individuals in order to fortify and strengthen the American economy over the long-term. Instead, Colorado Democrats passed HB20-1420 and undermined the bipartisan, Trump-initiated federal government's recovery assistance by enacting *additional* taxes on businesses, estates and trusts.

Here are a few of the changes that were made in regards to the CARES Act and the corresponding section found in HB20-1420:

- Section 2(1) net operating loss deduction as determined under Section 172(a) of the IRS relative to the CARES Act *eliminated;*
- Section 2(m) excess business loss as determined under Section 461(2) of the IRS deductions relative to the CARES Act *eliminated*;

- Section 2(n) excess of the limitation on business interest under section 163(j)relative to the CARES Act *eliminated*;
- Section (2).0 *repealed* a deduction allowed under Section 199A of the IRS code, which originated in the 2017 federal Tax Cuts & Jobs Act. It repeals for many businesses the 20% taxable income deduction for Colorado income taxes.

Referencing these few sections clearly exhibits the complexity of the bill.

The true winner in terms of monetary benefits will be tax accountants, as businesses seek assistance in filing tax returns correctly. It is well-recognized that legislators rarely consider the cost of compliance to businesses when passing complicated bills.

One interesting footnote to this far-reaching tax legislation: The final legislative Fiscal Note for HB20-1420 was not released until July 28, 2020, thirty-nine days *after* the bill was voted on by our elected representatives in both chambers, and seventeen days after the governor added his signature.[4]

Other financial winners of the bill will be state employment and state contractors. State contractors will be needed for computer programming, and computer and related testing, to name a few additional state expenditures. It is expected that 8.5 full time employees will be hired at a cost of approximately $424,000 within the Department of Revenue starting Fiscal Year 2021-22.

You might think that the bill also flies in the face of the Taxpayer's Bill of Rights (TABOR), because it clearly increases Colorado state taxes. Shouldn't voters have the right to give their consent or disapproval at the ballot box? Actually, not, according to current court interpretations of TABOR. If a tax credit (or "tax expenditure" in the Democrat lexicon) is created by statute, it can also be reduced or eliminated by act of the legislature without voter approval. Citizens may challenge the repeal or reduction of a tax credit by a lawsuit, but success in Colorado courts would be unlikely.

One final interesting footnote that speaks volumes about the tactics used in the packaging and enactment of HB20-1420. Four months before the bill's introduction at the end of May, on January 30, Democrats had introduced HB20-1203, "*EITC Earned Income Tax Credit And Child Tax Credit And Income Definition*.[5] In important respects, conceptually it was the precursor to 1420. but surprisingly attracted little notice or vocal opposition among Republicans. HB20-1203 passed the House Finance Committee on March 2, but then fell victim to the coronavirus recess in mid-March. When the legislature returned ten weeks later, Democrats introduced HB20-1420, a more radical bill designed to raise business taxes even more than 1203.

The disruption to a business' daily operation that began with the Governor's March shutdown orders continues with the upheavals set in motion by business legislation enacted by House and Senate Democrats. Ironically, the hoped-for additional tax revenue will not be generated from HB20-1420, as Colorado businesses will continue to disappear along with their jobs, and state expenditures will continue rise.

The *Denver Business Journal* reported in mid-August:

> *Some numbers can tell the story of what life has been like for one of the state's most important industries — restaurants employed one in every 12 Coloradans and*

> *generated $12 billion in sales in 2019— since coronavirus invaded. A full 91% of eateries laid off or furloughed workers in March or April, according to the Colorado Restaurant Association. An estimated 173,000 workers have lost jobs. Five of every six restaurants are operating below 50% capacity under newly imposed state restrictions.*[6]

The mastery of "double speak" by the Democrats is impressive. On the one hand, the business community met Democrat leadership through conference calls and Zoom meetings to keep the conversations open on business issues during the prolonged recess. As a result, business organizations were led to believe that their dire, highly volatile situation was being understood and reasonably assessed by the Democrat majority.

However, business leaders quickly learned the Democrat leadership actually had another plan of action: *increased taxation, not tax relief.*

All across Colorado, business owners and employees, and hundreds of communities served by them and dependent on them for tax revenue, are finding it hard to understand why the Democrat controlled House and Senate forced tax increases during a time when owners under extreme duress were terminating employees and downsizing due to the Governor's shut down orders. Even the state's progressive Governor has more than once remarked how stupid it is to raise taxes during a recession. The amazing short-sightedness and abuse of power that was the hallmark of the 2020 legislative session only exacerbates the challenges faced by tens of thousands businesses as their very existence is threatened.

NOTES

1. *2018 Small Business Profile, U.S. Small Business Administration Office of Advocacy: Colorado Small Business Profile, 2018.*
https://www.sba.gov/sites/default/files/advocacy/2018-Small-Business-Profiles-CO.pdf

2. *HB20-1420 Concerning the adjustment of certain state tax expenditures*
https://leg.colorado.gov/sites/default/files/2020a_1420_signed.pdf

3. *The CARES Act Works for All Americans.* U. S. Department of the Treasury
https://home.treasury.gov/policy-issues/cares

4. *HB20-1420 Final Fiscal Note*, Legislative Council Staff
https://leg.colorado.gov/sites/default/files/documents/2020A/bills/fn/2020a_hb1420_f1.pdf

5. HB20-1203 Colorado General Assembly
https://leg.colorado.gov/bill-search?search_api_views_fulltext=HB20-1203

6. Sealover, Ed. *Economy of Scale – Why Colorado restaurants will never be the same – if they survive at all. Denver Business Journal* August 20, 2020
https://www.bizjournals.com/denver/news/2020/08/20/denver-restaurants-coronavirus-tipping-staffing.html?ana=e_me_set1&j=90524647&t=Morning&mkt_tok=eyJpIjoiTVROak5qWTFOelZtTm1FMCI

10

FAMILIES AND CHILDREN: COLLATERAL DAMAGE IN THE CULTURE WAR?

BY JEFF HUNT
Leader of a Colorado Think Tank

How are Colorado families doing? Why is this important to discuss in a book about public policy? It's rather quite simple. When the family fails, the government steps in to provide services. For example, a two-parent, stable home is much less likely to be in poverty than a single-parent home. When a family is suffering from poverty, it requires considerably more government resources. If we want to limit government, and more importantly, see children in Colorado thriving, we must have healthy families.

There is good news and bad news regarding the health of Colorado families. Colorado parents, on the whole, are fantastic. Most kids trust their parents, feel they can approach their parents, and believe their parents are looking out for their best interests. The bad news is that there are fewer and fewer families, and many Colorado children face serious challenges from bullying, alcohol, drug abuse, and suicide.

Fewer Coloradans are getting married and having children. The marriage rate in Colorado is declining from 9.8 to 7.6 per 1,000 total population.[1] Since less people are getting married, the divorce rate has also declined from 5.5 to 3.3 per 1,000 total population.[2]

According to the Centers for Disease Control, the number of births per 1,000 females aged 15–44, declined from 2017 to 2018 by 4% to 6% in 10 states, including Colorado.[3] Colorado's abortion rate has dropped by 10% between 2014 and 2017 while the use of birth control has increased.[4]

So, in other words, fewer Coloradans are getting married, and the number of births are declining. Perhaps linked to this, Colorado remains relatively low on teen births compared to other states.[5] It also ranks nearly the best in the country for low percentage of births to unmarried mothers.[6] While both of these statistics look promising, a closer analysis shows problems.

Many of these statistics are indicative that Colorado is not building strong family structures; in fact, we are going the wrong direction. Yes, we have fewer abortions, fewer divorces, and fewer teen pregnancies, but those may be causally linked to a higher use of birth control, fewer marriages, and fewer children being born.

As conservatives who believe that traditional family structures are critical to a healthy society, we would prefer to see the marriage rate increasing, the number of births increasing, with the number of divorces, teen pregnancies, and abortions decreasing.

For Colorado children, most of the parents are invested in

their children and their future. According to the Healthy Kids Colorado Survey[7] a strong majority of kids in Colorado feel the rules in their family are clear, have chances to do fun things with their parents, have parents who know if they are not home on time, could ask their parents for help with a personal problem, and have parents that ask if their homework is done.

Unfortunately, these kids are facing serious challenges regarding bullying, alcohol use, drug use and suicide. The same study noted, "34.7% of students are feeling depressed, up from 31.4% in 2017."[8] Colorado had the highest increase in the teen suicide rate in the U.S. since 2016.[9]

On marijuana drug use, teens are moving from smoking marijuana to dabbing and vaping, which often results in using higher TCH potency pot.

Is the Colorado legislature doing anything to support and strengthen families? Quite the opposite. Instead, they are directly weakening the essential bonds between parents and children.

Conservatives believe that society operates best when the government is limited and most social services are provided by faith communities, social volunteer organizations, and healthy families. Over the past few decades, far-left radicals have done an excellent job removing faith communities and social volunteer programs from the public square in order to expand government. Who is best equipped to help the poor? Who is best equipped to educated children?

In cases like these, our society is relying more and more upon "government-certified experts" to provide these services. Unfortunately, as we've seen with both examples listed above, society is not getting better. Homeless populations are not dwindling, drug use is on the rise, and educational achievement levels in government-run public schools have stalled.

At one point in American history, the prime service provider of health care, education, and social services was the church. Our faith communities not only provided physical care to people in need, they provided important spiritual guidance as well. Consider this: since President Lyndon B. Johnson's war on poverty was initiated in 1965, the United States has spent three times more money combating poverty than all the wars since the American Revolution combined. The result? Almost no change in America's poverty rate.[10]

The radical far-left now has its sights on reducing a family's impact in directing the upbringing of a child. Just like with social services, they believe "government-certified experts" should be raising your children instead of you.

The far-left is not above board in their hostility towards parents; rarely do they let this show. Instead, they disguise their agenda in noble causes such as promoting equality, preventing suicide, improving mental health, and helping a child embrace his or her "true sexual identity."

There are several examples of laws recently passed and signed by Governor Polis that prove this point. Rather than strengthening families, these programs weaken families. Rather than empowering parents, they seek to usurp parents' role with a "government-certified expert." In the next few sections, I'll explore two of these laws and how they demonstrate a government takeover of traditional, healthy family roles.

HB19-1032 - Comprehensive Human Sexuality Education

One of the most controversial bills in 2019 was HB 19-1032, Comprehensive Human Sexuality Education. This legislation drew hundreds of families to testify in opposition. The Centennial Institute alone sent 2,800 letters to Colorado legislators in opposition to the bill.

HOUSE BILL 19-1032

BY REPRESENTATIVE(S) Lontine and Caraveo, Arndt, Bird, Buckner, Buentello, Coleman, Cutter, Duran, Esgar, Froelich, Galindo, Gonzales-Gutierrez, Hansen, Herod, Hooton, Jackson, Jaquez Lewis, Kennedy, Kipp, McCluskie, Melton, Michaelson Jenet, Mullica, Roberts, Singer, Sirota, Snyder, Tipper, Valdez A., Weissman, Becker, Titone; also SENATOR(S) Todd and Coram, Bridges, Court, Danielson, Fenberg, Fields, Ginal, Gonzales, Lee, Pettersen, Rodriguez, Story, Winter.

CONCERNING COMPREHENSIVE HUMAN SEXUALITY EDUCATION, AND, IN CONNECTION THEREWITH, MAKING AN APPROPRIATION.

Supported by Planned Parenthood and the American Civil Liberties Union (ACLU), HB 19-1032 allowed a further leftist takeover of sex education in public, government-run schools. Bottom line: because of this new law, if you teach sex-education in your school, you must teach it according to the dictates of the arch-leftist, Boulder-dominated Colorado legislature.

Believing the legislature had enough votes to get it passed, the Centennial Institute spent hundreds of hours working to limit this bill to older students, and getting as many opt-outs for parents and charter schools as we could. The original legislation allowed conversations on LGBTQ issues to be made with children as young as kindergartners. It also did not provide any opt-outs for charter schools.

HB19-1032, as signed by Governor Polis, requires that comprehensive sex education be "culturally sensitive." This is defined in the statute as "experiences and needs of communities of color; immigrant communities; lesbian, gay, bisexual, and transgender communities; PEOPLE WHO ARE INTERSEX".[11] The statute signed by the Governor is silent on "cultural sensitivity" to Christian, Jewish, or Muslim communities.

The original language had this interesting requirement: "Human sexuality instruction must not explicitly or implicitly teach or endorse religious ideology or sectarian tenets or doctrine." In other words, the state is mandating that sex education include the "experiences and needs" of lesbian, gay, bisexual, and transgender communities while explicitly banning "religious ideology."

Leftist perspectives on sex education embraced, religious perspectives rejected.

We were successful in removing the language banning the teaching of religious ideology, or traditional family values, we prevented kindergartners through third grade from having to face this type of leftist indoctrination, and we provided important opt-outs for charter schools.

The final bill included this language: Nothing in subsection (6) or (6.5) of this section shall be interpreted to prohibit discussion of health, moral, ethical, or religious values as they pertain to comprehensive human sexuality, healthy relationships, or family formation. SUCH DISCUSSION IS ENCOURAGED.

The bill as passed and signed by the governor is a continued step to remove parents out of the sex education process. This past session, a state senator ran a bill requiring stronger parental notification when it comes to what sex education is being taught to our children in government-run schools. His bill, SB20-072, "requires an electronic notification to be provided to the parent or legal guardian of each student, in addition to the written notification, 90 days prior to commencing the planned curriculum. The notification must include the date the planned curriculum will be taught and it must be sent separately from any other school notifications. Any materials used during the planned curriculum must be made available for viewing online 90 days prior to the commencement of the planned curriculum".[12]

The favorable senate bill died in committee along a party-line vote; Democrats unanimously opposed it. All this bill did was help parents better understand what is being taught to their children regarding sex education.

After sitting through hours and hours of testimony on HB19-1032 and then SB20-072, it is clear the primary goal of leftists was to continue to remove parents from conversations regarding their child's sex education.

What is now taught in Colorado's government-run public schools regarding sex education is entirely dominated by leftist, pro-LGBTQ, pro-choice curriculum. There is no evidence this approach to comprehensive sex education is working for the benefit of children, families or society.

On top of this, the legislature refuses to provide adequate notification for parents regarding what is being taught to their children. As mentioned earlier, Colorado's radical, far-left officials believe they have a better, "more inclusive" approach to sex education, and they will fight to control what is being taught to your children.

While the comprehensive sex education bill was an atrocious abuse of parental rights, it pales in comparison to the real damage done by HB19-1120, concerning multiple approaches to prevent youth suicide.

HB19-1120 - Youth Mental Health Education And Suicide Prevention

Colorado faces a youth suicide epidemic. Unfortunately, in a proposed effort to reduce youth suicide, HB19-1120allows an unlimited number of meetings between a school counselor and a child as young as 12 *without parental notification*. Parents are a critical component in helping children confront mental health issues. HB19-1120 is a violation of parental rights and may do further harm to children by not involving parents in a child's care.

Just imagine that your teenage daughter is struggling with depression. At home, she is fine and doesn't indicate any symptoms. At school, she is meeting with a counselor regularly to discuss a variety of issues, including her depression. Because of this law, a parent may never know that these meetings are taking place.

Similar to HB19-1032, I sat through hours of testimony listening to the proponents. You would think that the greatest harm to a child struggling with depression were the parents. Leftist legislators promoting this bill believe that "government-certified counselors" are not only the best equipped to help a child, but the *only* people that should be helping a child.

HB19-1032 and HB19-1120 were direct attacks on the sacred, God-given bond between parents and children: First, to be able to instill a family's values regarding sex education, and second, to be the primary caregiver to a child suffering from mental health issues.

It is pure arrogance that drives government leaders to interrupt this sacred bond by removing parents from the equation, so "government-certified experts" driven by leftist, secular, and often nihilist values can raise our society's children. Thousands of parents in 2019 fought hard against these new laws and in the 2020 legislative session, Colorado Republican legislators attempted to roll back these abuses on parental rights.

Parents Bill of Rights

People often ask me what the next frontier of battles against the radical left will be. We all know that religious freedom battles have dominated the headlines. Back in 2006, when I worked for Senator Rick Santorum, there were only a few Senators and Representatives even working on religious freedom issues.

The next frontier of battles against the radical left will include defending the God-given rights of parents. In 2020, a group of conservative legislators introduced HB20-1144, which establishes a Colorado parent's bill of rights. This bill sets forth specific parental rights related to directing the upbringing, education, and health care of a minor child[13].

Tragically, the bill died along a party-line vote in committee as leftist special-interest groups showed up to testify that parents are not best suited to raise their own children.

Not All Doom and Gloom

The Colorado legislature did have one moment in 2019 of bi-partisan support towards crisis pregnancies with the passing of Senate Bill 25, Information to Students Regarding Safe Haven Laws. This requires the teaching of Safe Haven opportunities to teenagers who face an unwanted pregnancy. Rather than abandoning a child, they can safely drop a child off at a fire station, hospital, community center, etc.

There are moments, albeit rare, when the Colorado legislature embraces the sanctity of life.

Ballot Initiatives

Outside of the legislature, ballot initiatives continue to weaken family structures. Since 2012, Colorado has passed initiatives that include the commercialization of marijuana, doctor-assisted suicide, and online sports betting.

The combining of Colorado's liberal and libertarian voters have allowed some of the ballot initiatives to pass with large margins. Unfortunately, the world-view that is allowing these ballot proposals to be successful is driven more by a radical individualism that mistakes freedom for license.

The conservative world-view never allows for a radical notion of freedom: drug-use, prostitution, gambling, doctor-assisted suicide, etc. First of all, we reject any notion that an act can be purely individual. One choosing to do drugs in his basement doesn't just harm the individual: it effects the family and community at large. The person using drugs doesn't work as well (it affects companies), he doesn't drive well (it affects commuters), he doesn't care for his children as well (it affects his family), he makes less money and pays fewer taxes (it affects tax revenue). The institution that God established is the family, and we must look at Colorado's ballot initiatives through the lens of how it affects the family institution. Does the ballot initiative create stronger or weaker families?

Secondly, we reject a definition of freedom that believes mankind is free to do whatever it pleases. That is not freedom, it's license. Freedom is grounded in God's definition of freedom. When someone engages in drug use and gambling, they are not practicing freedom. More often than not, they are shackling their freedom. Is a person who loses money in a casino regularly or uses drugs regularly truly free? No. They are in bondage to their addictions.

In Edmund Burke's letter to a Member of the National Assembly of France in 1791, he said,

> *"Men are qualified for civil liberty in exact proportion to their disposition to put moral chains upon their own appetites, — in proportion as their love to justice is above their rapacity, — in proportion as their soundness and sobriety of understanding is above their vanity and presumption, — in proporton as they are more disposed to listen to the counsels of the wise and good, in preference to the flattery of knaves. Society cannot exist, unless a controlling power upon will and appetite be placed somewhere; and the less of it there is within, the more there must be without. It is ordained in the eternal constitution of*

> *things, that men of intemperate minds cannot be free. Their passions forge their fetters."*

One of the critical lines in Burke's letter is, "*the less of it there is within, the more there must be without*." Self-control is critical to a limited government. The less self-control, the more government control is required. The ballot initiatives listed above expand vice, result in greater government control, and, most importantly, weaken the family.

For Colorado families to thrive, Colorado must reject misguided ballot initiatives that expand destructive vices.

How to fight back

Similar to how conservatives and religious communities worked to protect religious freedom, conservatives in Colorado must be able to argue and litigate successfully on behalf of parental rights.

Parents are the best equipped to raise their children; even the children say so. Unfortunately, a radical legislature and governor, controlled by leftist, secular, nihilistic special interests like Planned Parenthood, are working to further remove parents from the role of raising children. This must be rejected and actively opposed. Conservatives must support efforts by legislators to pass a Parents Bill of Rights. Furthermore, we must speak out against a state that's embracing ballot initiatives detrimental to healthier families.

If we want limited government, safe communities, excellent schools, and a strong economy, put families first!

NOTES

1. *CDC/NCHS – Marriage rates by State: 1990, 1995, and 1999-2018*
https://www.cdc.gov/nchs/data/dvs/state-marriage-rates-90-95-99-

18.pdf

2. *CDC/NCHS – Divorce rates by State: 1990, 1995, and 1999-2018* https://www.cdc.gov/nchs/data/dvs/state-divorce-rates-90-95-99-18.pdf

3. *Births: Final Data for 2018. National Vital Statistics Reports Volume 68, Number 13.* November 27, 2019. https://www.cdc.gov/nchs/data/nvsr/nvsr68/nvsr68_13-508.pdf

4. Brown, Jennifer. *Colorado abortion rates keep declining. Free IUDs and easier access to the pill are the reason.* The Colorado Sun. October 21, 2019 https://coloradosun.com/2019/10/21/colorado-abortion-rates-keep-declining-free-iuds-and-easier-access-to-the-pill-are-the-reason/

5. *CDC Teen Birth Rate by State National Center for Health Statistics* https://www.cdc.gov/nchs/pressroom/sosmap/teen-births/teenbirths.htm

6. *Percentage of Births to Unmarried Mothers by State. Centers for Disease Control and Prevention (CDC)* https://www.cdc.gov/nchs/pressroom/sosmap/unmarried/unmarried.htm

7. *Healthy Kids Colorado Survey.* Colorado Department of Public Health & Environment. https://www.colorado.gov/pacific/cdphe/healthy-kids-colorado-survey-data

8. Chavira, Danielle. *More Colorado Students Feeling Depressed, Know Vaping Is Risky, Survey Finds.* CBS Denver. August 3, 2020 https://denver.cbslocal.com/2020/08/03/colorado-student-health-survey/

8. Daley, John. *The rate of Teen Suicide in Colorado Increased by 58% in 3 Years, Making it The Cause of 1 in 5 Adolescent Deaths.* CPR News September 17, 2019. https://www.cpr.org/2019/09/17/the-rate-of-teen-suicide-in-colorado-increased-by-58-percent-in-3-1.years-making-it-the-cause-of-1-in-5-adolescent-deaths/

10. Rector, Robert. *Commentary Marriage and Family — The War on Poverty: 50 Years of Failure.* Heritage.org

September 23, 2014
https://www.heritage.org/marriage-and-family/commentary/the-war-poverty-50-years-failure

11. HB19-1032 General Assembly of the State of Colorado
signed 5/31/2019
https://leg.colorado.gov/sites/default/files/2019a_1032_signed.pdf

12. *SB20-072 Human Sexuality Education Notification Requirement* – did not pass
https://leg.colorado.gov/bills/sb20-072

13. *HB20-1144 Parent's Bill of Rights — did not pass*
https://leg.colorado.gov/bills/hb20-1144

11

PROGRESSIVES' CONTINUING WAR ON AGRICULTURE AND RURAL COLORADO

BY JERRY SONNENBERG
Colorado State Senator

The challenges that rural Colorado faces are as vivid and varied as the terrain of Colorado itself – and that's without the complications, obstacles, and immense pressures placed on the state's rural regions by an overreaching and urban-centered "progressive" government.

Colorado is divided into sixty-four counties, of which a whopping fifty-three counties are home and hearth to 20% of the state's population. These citizens have a limited voice at the state capitol: just four of the thirty-five state Senators represent 73% of Colorado's land mass, and as one might imagine, their voices are often drowned out by the noise of the thirty-one urban, suburban, and ski town legislators. Now, add the ambitions of both a governor who does not understand – nor cares to learn about – rural issues, and those of increasingly left-of-center state government agencies, and the impact of the government's deliberate anti-rural policies are amplified.

'Rural Colorado'   Photo by C.V. Kirkstadt

For decades, people worried about judges overstepping their roles by legislating from the bench. In fact, judges turning court-issued decisions into rules and regulations is a well-documented occurrence, which rightly inflamed the debate of the separation of powers within the three branches of government. Now, during this time of unprecedented economic dislocations and great uncertainty, that power snatch has shifted into a different danger zone.

Our radical governor has selected agency heads who will execute his radical agenda

Through appointments and executive orders, our radical left Governor is very comfortable legislating from the executive mansion, and our Democrat-led legislature appears comfortable letting him do it. Colorado's legislative branch meets a limited number of days each year, and in 2020,

Colorado lawmakers chose to suspend its session, while over two dozen administrative agencies and commissions were allowed to continue to generate costly new rules and regulations. While the decision to allow administrative agencies to continue their work may appear responsible, it seems almost insidious to allow agencies to create rules at a time when none of the public is allowed to oversee the rulemaking process. Further, there is an inherent problem with ceding rulemaking power from legislators who are accountable to the public to agencies who are not. You may say, well, these executive agencies are accountable to the governor. To which I reply: Gimme a break!

When Governor Polis signed his Declaration of a public health emergency on March 11, the clear inability for the public to be in the room and be heard in a normal rulemaking process should have led to a suspension of all rulemaking proceedings for the duration of the emergency. Instead, the rulemaking process continued undeterred, with far less public or stakeholder involvement than ever before.

These rulemaking bodies are often several layers removed from anyone amenable to the public, and seldom is the agencies' ultimate boss — the governor — held responsible for the regulations put in place. In fact, for years rules have been increasingly adopted and implemented with little input from Colorado citizens. To attend multiple public hearings in a typical rulemaking process can be a daunting task; even if one manages to scour the internet to find the information, the often far-off locations of these meetings provides an even greater challenge for those who reside in rural areas of the state.

During my first term in the Colorado House over a decade ago, then-Minority Leader Mike May told me, "If you don't vote your district, they will find somebody who will!" In my fourteen years serving in the legislative branch since then, I have done my best to fight for my constituents on the issues that truly matter to rural Coloradans. Elected officials ultimately answer to their constituents, the voters, which dictates the kind of laws they support and regulations they authorize. After lawmakers pass new laws, various agencies are tasked with creating rules to ensure a smooth transition into the enactment.

In the textbook version of this process, an agency's rulemaking is prescribed by both the letter and the spirit of the statutes they are meant to implement. If the lawmakers who passed the statute have conscientiously represented the constituents who will be impacted by the agency-made rules implementing the newly-passed law, there will be few surprises. However, since the Democratic majority of lawmakers who control the bills passed in today's General Assembly have little interest in understanding or representing rural values and interests, the smooth, rational rulemaking system described in textbooks bears little resemblance to reality.

The current public health crisis has amplified this ongoing problem with the operations of the executive branch in our state government, especially in rural counties. Hardly anyone operating a farm or a small business of any kind in our rural areas believes the governor and his state government bureaucracy are looking out for their interests.

Governor Polis has increased his ability to implement a radical agenda statewide through his appointments to boards and commissions. His appointees are deliberately creating burdensome new rules and regulations, often far beyond what was contemplated by the lawmakers who sponsored the underlying legislation. These appointments have become a powerful tool to further an agenda that most Coloradans do not support and never voted for. The increasing reliance on agency-generated rules and regulations never put before the voters amounts to a hijacking of public policy priorities for increasingly radical purposes. The appointments being made by our governor can and will move the needle on a political agenda much more quickly — and with much less public involvement — than through a legislative process more open to political debate, media scrutiny, and public input.

The agenda of an activist Governor pushing his left-leaning policies over the cliff is exemplified by the recent appointment of a self-proclaimed vegan activist to the State Board of Veterinary Medicine. This board oversees veterinarians that both our urban and suburban cousins utilize when their favorite cat or dog gets sick as well as those the farmers and ranchers call on to nurse a sick animal back to health.

It is fair to ask, what can a vegan *activist* bring to the oversight of a *State Veterinary Board*? An activist who denounces the ownership of animals, even the family dog? Someone who despises the entire industry of livestock agriculture, which is so central to our state's economy, history, and way of life? One's menu choices are a personal matter; no argument from me. But introducing a person whose agenda is to destroy the relationship of man's best friend and an entire industry against the will of the public is far from a private lifestyle choice. This activist even made a statement on social media professing to care more about an electrocuted bird than the fire it started in Douglas County and the possible destruction of personal property that might have occurred, but for the brave firefighters who took action to prevent such a tragedy. It is very likely this vegan activist appointee will conscientiously push an anti-livestock agenda; and pardon me, but it does not take a policy wizard to see that doesn't play well in rural Colorado.

The problems with Governor Polis' appointments go beyond just the people he has chosen. He has left entire regions with little to no representation on these state boards and commissions. Of the 220 appointments he has made thus far to 25 boards or commissions that affect rural Colorado, only 12 – less than 6%! – were from rural areas east of the Interstate 25 urban corridor.

Some boards and commissions have been mandated by state statutes to contain appointees from each Congressional District; the State Fair Board is an example of one such board. Presumably, the goal is to pull from the knowledge of the entire state in order to cover the expertise needed to put a struggling fair on the track to success. The 4th Congressional District comprises all of the eastern plains plus Longmont, in the corner of Boulder County. In the 2020 legislative session, the appointment from that district did not come from anywhere on the vast expanse of the eastern plains but indeed from the Governor's own home county. That appointee's credentials to govern the State Fair were that he oversaw a farmers market. Now, there might be a correlation there somewhere, but I just can't see how that limited expertise is helpful in pulling the State Fair back from the brink of bankruptcy.

The State Fair is more than a collection of produce stands; it includes a complex system of housing, showing, and judging live animals, none of which are standard at a local farmers market. The governor's appointment seems a little like putting a kid from the sandbox in charge of a construction site. This obviously inappropriate appointment has garnered bipartisan opposition, but political games and sidestepping has allowed this appointee to continue to serve in an "interim capacity."

Previous governors' gun control and mandated energy choices were bad enough, and some of their quoted beliefs about "backwards thinking" rural Coloradans are nothing short of condescending and arrogant, but even they tried to keep some sort of political balance. Governor Polis, with his disregard of any interests outside of his own high-handed activism, has us wondering when this war on rural Colorado will end.

Not only does this governor ignore the eastern plains in his appointment-making, he does not even try to conceal his political prejudice. By his appointments, the State Fair Board has been restructured to make it a politically biased board with six Democrat appointees, three politically unaffiliated, and a single Republican. It has become very apparent that this governor doesn't believe that someone with an "R" by their name can have valid ideas and contributions. And, in light of his regional bias against rural areas, it appears that living on the eastern plains precludes even a Democrat from being fit for service on this governor's boards and commissions.

Even water conservation has become a political football

Surely, one might think, the hostility of Colorado's progressive governor towards rural Colorado would not extend to its life blood, water. Well, think again.

A ready supply of clean water is essential to not only agriculture but to the region's small communities. The expanding areas along the front range demand more and more water to meet the needs of that booming population. Unfortunately, at this point the only place to draw the water they need is to take it from rural areas, which inevitably means to draw from agriculture's water supply. Agriculture owns the rights to use roughly 80% of the state's water, and there is currently a "buy and dry" procedure that transplants the water from a rural plot of land to the water-thirsty front range cities, leaving a brittle and lifeless landscape behind.

Mural located on the first floor of the rotunda of the Colorado State Capitol

One obvious solution to prevent further devastation of the "buy and dry" practice is to build more storage. Would you believe that over the past decade the primary obstacle to building more reservoir capacity has been the environmental lobby – whose headquarters are (of course) in Boulder, far removed from the rural areas in desperate need of more water storage.

Our need to keep Colorado's water in Colorado should be forefront in our policy discussions. During the last ten years or so, we have allowed an average of approximately 300,000 acre/feet of water to flow out of our state beyond our compact on the South Platte River. That is enough water to provide for 675,000 new homes in urban settings – water that could be used to satisfy not only our urban growth but take the pressure off of our rural communities and agriculture. We can do that right now through storage, either by building new dams or reservoirs, expanding current storage facilities, or even using underground closed basins.

The environmental community continues to push back on any storage using delay tactics and law suits. The Northern Integrated Supply Project — a water storage plan that would provide much-needed water for fifteen communities in northern Colorado — has been tied up by activists for nearly twenty years. Communities that need water for new homes being built for the influx of people who have fallen in love with our great state are forced to take water from agriculture because we are prevented from storing our water in plentiful times to use in times of drought. Leading the charge against water storage in Colorado is none other than environmental activists who made millions selling craft beer from Fort Collins, who have given no thought in their crusade against agriculture to the rural communities who depend on the ag industry. A true environmentalist would be fighting back against the artificial desertification and the devastation of the great plains.

Governor Polis' activism has also bled into the government and the agencies that oversee our water. Agencies such as Colorado Department of Public Health and Environment (CDPHE) continuously move the bar on water quality standards, forcing small communities to spend money they do not have in order to change their water quality systems.

One such community has been drinking the same water since

their wells were put in place decades ago, when the acceptable amount of a specific chemical in the water was 2.75 nanograms. A nanogram is roughly equal to one drop of water in twenty Olympic size swimming pools – so two-and-three-quarter drops in those twenty pools. Then the CDPHE in their infinite wisdom lessened the acceptable amount by half of a drop of water in those Olympic sized swimming pools, and this town had to spend $30 million to correct this infinitesimal discrepancy. Taxpayers footed the bill through higher fees, and now the most burdensome utility cost for a homeowner in that small community is water.

These changes don't come from legislation; they come from rulemaking and regulations put forward from activist boards and commissions appointed by the governor.

The Water Quality Control Commission is within CDPHE and as the name implies, regulates water quality in Colorado. More than 80% of the state's water is used for agriculture and most of the ag production in Colorado is on the eastern plains, so one might think that there would be several quality appointments from that part of the state– but you would be wrong. There is just one person who was appointed in 2020 from LaJunta, and everyone else is from the front range or the west slope. Thus, the vast majority of the communities affected by this commission's decisions do not have a voice to represent their needs and interests.

Another powerful commission is the Colorado Parks and Wildlife Commission. Again, with a large number of state parks in eastern Colorado and nearly a million acres of public walk-in areas for hunting and fishing, you would think that there would be representation from the eastern third of the state. Again, you would be wrong. While it is important not to discount the large animal wildlife populations in need of management west of the urban corridor, a significant amount of hunting occurs on the eastern plains, where hunters of both large animal wildlife such as deer and pronghorn as well as the smaller fowl and animal species abound.

There are thirteen members of the CPW Commission, and just one appointee from Wray was made to represent the eastern plains. However, that single representative of the eastern plains had just moved to Wray after being a Jackson County Commissioner through the beginning of 2019. How can a person who had lived in the mountains for the previous twenty years be the voice of all of the eastern plains regarding hunting, fishing, and state parks issues? We all know one size does not fit all and her experience with these issues in the mountains are a size different than the issues faced on the plains.

Production agriculture is also a target

Believe it or not, it gets even worse for rural Colorado. The Colorado Parks and Wildlife Commission is required to appoint three members to their commission to represent production agriculture — the purpose of which is ensure that the commission will have the expertise and understanding to address issues like damage caused by wildlife on farmers' property, and how agriculture can work side-by-side with recreation. At the same time that a mountain-to-plains transplant appointee was announced, so was an agriculture representative from Aspen. This appointee runs an organization that teaches sustainable living workshops to all ages, builds edible gardens and compost systems for individuals and communities, and hosts community events, meals, and festivals. Draw your own conclusion, but it looks to many that the Polis administration is tilting all scales away from production agriculture. To borrow a phrase from current "social justice" movements, representation matters, and this governor lacks the desire to ensure that one third of our state is truly represented.

Hints of this governor's disdain for farmers and ranchers were evident in statements that misrepresented agriculture, through public promotions for burgers made from something other than meat, and in his incorrect statements about animal antibiotics during COVID-19 briefings. His utter disinterest in understanding the business makes it clear that his agenda lies outside of protecting and encouraging production agriculture, and his "vegan activist" appointee seems to indicate an unsettling dislike for the industry.

The governor's favorite target is the oil and gas industry

Perhaps most troubling of all, this Boulder progressive governor, has also shown that he cares little for the state's economic well-being. Essentially, there are two major economic industries in rural Colorado: agriculture, which touts over $40 billion in receipts annually, and oil and gas production, which has nearly the same economic impact.

This administration's obvious hatred towards the fossil fuel industry will not only destroy local communities that rely on these companies and their workers, it will in time destroy the state and local governments' budgets.

Fossil fuel companies that operate in Colorado pay large amounts of property taxes, which then fund schools and other essential programs in those counties. These companies also pay state severance taxes that fund a whole litany of services. The loss of property taxes to the local communities will mean that the state will have to back-fill those losses with money they will not have, because the state's portion of oil and gas taxes has been reduced as well. Thus, the government-mandated decline in oil and gas industry generated revenues will create an endless cycle of debts and defaults, in which the real victims will be the very communities that environmental extremists claim to be protecting.

Governor Polis' plot to end oil and gas is a blow to the entire state. His conspiracy — which was in direct opposition to the will of the majority of Colorado's voters — was passed and implemented on a very short time line in the legislature in 2019 before being placed on the governor's desk. That legislation will be looked on in the very near future as one that changed the socioeconomic dynamic in Colorado forever. We have already seen bankruptcies of oil and gas companies, the sale of Colorado assets in that industry, and huge mergers as the only companies that may be able to weather the storm are international giants. The little guy that may have had a rig or two, or took a chance on a lease to build a business is gone forever, thanks to the governor's "progressive" agenda.

Rural Colorado is suffering the painful 'death by a thousand cuts'

But it is not just the farmers, ranchers, and the oil and gas economy he seems to be trying to destroy. It is a way of life – it's a community culture. Radical policy decisions have put rural Colorado in crisis. The fear of the death of our way of life by a thousand cuts is real, and it is terrifying to our small communities. The rift between rural and urban is growing, and that divide will only be intensified as this governor continues to push his radical agenda.

The environmental activists' scheme to introduce wolves and upset an already balanced ecosystem will prove to be a community divider – just like we saw in the communities built around coal, when policies meant to remove coal as one energy source of many in our toolbox were escalated. These pro-wolf, anti-coal policies are cut from the same cloth as those that ended the timber industry in Colorado, which in turn led to the unmanaged forests through which horrendous wildfires now blaze.

The harmful, offensive legislation that surfaced in the last two years shows a complete lack of understanding of how rural areas of the state function and succeed. Bills introduced to ban or restrict certain pesticides would set agriculture and soil and water conservation back 50 years – a clear slap in the face both to those who rely on the land for their livelihood and to the progress of science. In the first decade of our new century, it was actually hotter and drier than in the 'dirty 30s',yet the use of those pesticides prevented soil erosion and conserved enough water such that we did not see a return of the dust bowl. Nobody wants to see clouds of dust roaring across the plains again.

There have been bills to mandate working hours and conditions for farmers across Colorado — farmers who collect their paycheck once a year, during harvest, who run the race against Father Time to beat the great hail harvester in the sky. These farmers know to carry their water and to take breaks when time permits, but that a mandated five-minute water break every four hours in the shade with fresh water is unworkable. Eighteen-hour days are part-and-parcel with farming, but so are three or four consecutive days off when it has rained and the fields are unworkable. Agriculture doesn't work on the Gregorian calendar; it works with Mother Nature on her schedule, and agriculture has to be prepared to adapt to ever-changing conditions and weather. Government calendars have no place in the Colorado agriculture workplace, and the employees understand that.

Mental health is another major issue for many rural areas. Political decisions that take money from outlying counties high in mental health and drug issues per capita and place those dollars in areas along the front range are just another slice in the death by a thousand cuts.

You want to talk gun control? Those are fightin' words in rural Colorado. Those who call a pickup without a gun rack in the back window a 'tourist's truck' view any legislation to restrict the use of guns to be a clear violation of the second amendment. As far as I'm concerned, it goes without saying that they are right to be suspicious of anyone who seeks to curtail their constitutional rights.

As far as leadership during a crisis, this governor has consistently failed rural Colorado. His 100+ executive orders that have plagued Coloradans during this pandemic hit rural areas even harder. Rural parts of the state already systematically self-distance and protect each other, yet this governor has picked winners and losers through his executive orders. Small 'ma and pop' stores, the foundation of our small communities, were deemed non-essential, while the big box stores remained open and took business from hometown shops.

During the pandemic, I had to replace a failed freezer or lose all of the frozen food stored in there. My hometown appliance store was designated "non-essential" and could not be open, so my only option was the big box store. Many of those smaller 'ma and pop' shops will not reopen, nor the local restaurant that closed with a freezer full of food now unfit for preparation, the money invested in that small business wasted with its food.

While there was some agreement that actions should be taken during this pandemic, the uncertainty in the ever-changing data, with shifting calculations and inconsistent protection advice across the agencies, prevented any sort of definitive action. Governor Polis' neglect of rural Colorado became glaringly apparent when Denver offered free testing, even though rural nursing homes were unable to get the test kits they needed to keep our most vulnerable population safe.

Then Democratic lawmakers and the Mayor of Denver joined arms with the protestors and allowed them to gather in large groups – disregarding all COVID-19 health and safety mandates – while the governor's orders prevented law-abiding, God-fearing citizens from attending church. Well, that was the last straw for many Coloradans – and not all of them were farmers and cowboys.

The death of rural Colorado by a thousand cuts has been accelerated by the governor's deliberate severing of the right hand of the state, the oil and gas industry. Unfortunately, his escalating attacks on agriculture and the eastern plains may prove to be the final blow.

Part Three: What is to be Done?

When I shut up the heavens so that there is no rain, or command locusts to devour the land or send a plague among my people, if my people, who are called by my name, will humble themselves and pray and seek my face and turn from their wicked ways, then I will hear from heaven, and I will forgive their sin and will heal their land.

2 Chronicles 7:13-14

12

WHO WILL TELL THE PEOPLE? SACRIFICING THE STATE CONSTITUTION FOR A 30-YEAR CLIMATE POLICY YET TO BE MADE

BY PAUL SEBY
Environmental Regulations Attorney

While some proclaim it no longer "open to reasonable debate," the issue of "Climate Change" is a very complex one on which many Americans have differing opinions. That is no different in Colorado.

At the federal level, the topic has been the subject of several decades of consideration – ranging from the U.S. Senate's overwhelming rejection of the United States joining the Kyoto Protocol, the Congress' rejection of a cap and trade bill, the U.S. Supreme Court's halting President Obama's Clean Power Plan regulations, and the United States' rejection of the Paris Climate Accord. All of these actions were based on deep concerns over massive cost increases in electricity rates, harm to American manufacturing and jobs, disproportionate impacts on minority and fixed income citizens, and the EPA's own admissions that federal "greenhouse gas" (GHG) regulations would deliver minute or nonexistent effects on global temperatures.

These developments on the federal level have led to strong differences of opinion (and actions) in certain states. California, for example, has adopted many laws and policies motivated by its elected officials desire to reduce GHG emissions in that state. "It is one of the happy incidents of the federal system that a single courageous State may . . . try novel social and economic experiments without risk to the rest of the country.[1] Very recently, California has become an apparent model for certain politicians in Colorado.

While "federalism" is a fundamental pillar of American constitutionalism — so too is the separation of powers. So fundamental is that doctrine in the federal Constitution that States like Colorado incorporated it directly into its

Constitution upon admission as a State to the Union. The Colorado Constitution's separation of powers supplies a key bulwark for protecting the individual liberty of all Coloradans in the Centennial State.

This paper is an assessment of Colorado's new law enacted in 2019, *"Concerning the reduction of greenhouse gas pollution, and, in connection therewith, establishing statewide greenhouse gas pollution reduction goals and making an appropriation,"* and how it runs afoul of one of our state Constitution's most central features – the separation of power amongst the State's legislative, executive and judicial branches. In that statute, contrary to conventional lawmaking, instead of declaring an actual "law," the Colorado General Assembly merely declared "goals" for statewide reductions of Greenhouse Gases in Colorado (GHG's) over the next 30 years and then left the future translation of those "goals" into enforceable law to the seven unelected members of the Colorado Air Quality Commission (AQCC).

Why the Constitutional Separation of Powers Matters

The Founders of the United States of America were familiar with human nature and the correlative tendency of every ruler towards tyranny and realized that the only way to truly protect individual liberty was to limit the power of any single government official. James Madison, a central architect of the U.S. Constitution, rightly observed that if "men were angels, no government would be necessary."[2] He knew that every official or body would seek to accumulate "all powers, legislative, executive, and judiciary, in the same hands," and that such a concentration would be "the very definition of tyranny."[3] Thomas Jefferson agreed, labeling such a concentration of power as "precisely the definition of despotic government."[4] At the national level, the Founders addressed this tendency towards tyranny in specific ways. They recognized that the only way to limit each *official's* power was to limit each *office's* power – that is, to divide the sovereign power of government across different offices and separate branches. The Founders therefore divided federal power across three different branches and numerous different officials. They did so both to limit each individual official's unilateral power and to ensure that the People knew which of their elected officials to hold accountable for different governmental actions. The Founders created this system by dividing the government's powers among, and even within, three separate and competing branches.

This system cannot function, though, if the branches do not fulfill (or respect) their constitutionally-designated roles and jealously guard their prerogatives when other branches encroach. The separation of powers is a large part of why our Republic and our State have long endured.

The hope of this article is that it will shine a much needed light on the fact that a majority of Colorado's legislators, in 2019, agreed to allow their sole legislative authority under the Colorado Constitution to be reallocated (without limitation) to seven unelected members of the AQCC.

The Separation of Powers in the Colorado Constitution is the Foundation of Colorado's Democratic Form of Government.

The essential structural division of power into three branches created by the Colorado Constitution parallels that of our sister states and also that of the U.S. Constitution. Colorado courts consider these decisions as persuasive authority on principles of separation of powers, mindful that such principles are fundamental to the American system of government.

The Colorado Constitution creates three branches of government and vests each branch with a distinct type of power:

Colorado Const. art. III, § 1: "[T]he legislative power of this state shall be vested in a legislative assembly . . . .";

Colorado Const. art. V, § 1: "The executive power is vested in the governor . . . .";

Colorado Const. art. VI, § 1 : "The judicial power of the state is vested in a unified judicial system . . . ." .

By vesting each branch with a distinct form of power, the state Constitution keeps those powers separate. The three branches are "coequal," Colorado Const. art. XI, § 26, each "acting within its proper sphere is supreme."[5]

The Colorado Supreme Court has long recognized that the express formalization of separation of powers in Article XI, § 26 is an apportionment of power among three branches and implicitly excluded each branch from exercising the powers of the others: "nor can one [branch] directly interfere with the other in the performance of functions delegated by the Constitution"; *Board v. District Court*, 138 *Colo. 227, 232 (Colo. 1958)*. See also *Miller v. French*, 530 U.S. 327, 341 (2000), explaining that separation of powers doctrine "prohibits one branch from encroaching on the central prerogatives of another".

HB 19-1261 Violates the Colorado Constitution[6]

In 2019, the Colorado General Assembly enacted two bills, SB 19-096 and HB 19-1261, which gives the Colorado Air Quality Control Commission (AQCC) sweeping authority to inventory and regulate GHG emissions in Colorado. SB 19-096 establishes requirements for measuring and reporting GHG emissions from facilities (the "inventory"), and HB 19-1261 sets GHG emission reduction "goals" based on that inventory. Specifically, HB 19-1261 requires that Colorado shall reduce GHG pollution by 26% by 2025, 50% by 2030, and 90% by 2050 from the levels of GHG emissions that existed in 2005. (See Section 1; C.R.S. § 25-7-102(2)(g). It directs the AQCC to achieve these broad GHG reduction goals by implementing policies and promulgating rules to reduce GHG pollution. (See Section 3; C.R.S. § 25-7-105.)

HB 19-1261 added the following "Legislative Declaration."

> Accordingly, **Colorado shall** strive to increase renewable energy generation and eliminate statewide greenhouse gas pollution by the middle of the twenty-first century **and have goals of achieving, at a minimum, a twenty-six-percent reduction in statewide greenhouse gas pollution by 2025, fifty-percent reduction in statewide greenhouse gas pollution by 2030, and a ninety-percent reduction in statewide greenhouse gas pollution by 2050.** The reductions identified in this subsection 2(g) are measured relative to 2005 statewide greenhouse gas pollution levels. (CRS, §25-7-102(2)(g) [emphasis added]).

HOUSE BILL 19-1261

BY REPRESENTATIVE(S) Becker and Jackson, Jaquez Lewis, Bird, Cutter, Duran, Froelich, Galindo, Hooton, Kennedy, Kipp, Melton, Roberts, Singer, Sirota, Snyder, Sullivan, Tipper, Titone, Valdez A., Weissman, Arndt, Benavidez, Buckner, Buentello, Caraveo, Exum, Gonzales-Gutierrez, Gray, Hansen, Lontine, McCluskie, Michaelson Jenet, Mullica, Esgar, Herod, McLachlan;
also SENATOR(S) Winter and Williams A., Moreno, Bridges, Court, Danielson, Donovan, Fenberg, Fields, Foote, Ginal, Gonzales, Lee, Pettersen, Story, Todd, Zenzinger.

CONCERNING THE REDUCTION OF GREENHOUSE GAS POLLUTION, AND, IN CONNECTION THEREWITH, ESTABLISHING STATEWIDE GREENHOUSE GAS POLLUTION REDUCTION GOALS AND MAKING AN APPROPRIATION.

Further, in a fit of odd historical absent-mindedness, the legislation left it to the AQCC to determine what the 2005 levels of GHG *were* in Colorado.

> **"Statewide greenhouse gas pollution" means the total net statewide anthropogenic emissions** of carbon dioxide, methane, nitrous oxide, hydrofluorocarbons, perfluorocarbons, nitrogen trifluoride, and sulfur hexafluoride, expressed as carbon dioxide equivalent

> **calculated using a methodology and data** on radiative forcing and atmospheric persistence **deemed appropriate by the Commission**.
> (CRS, §25-7-103(22.5) [emphasis added]).

Then, the Colorado legislature added the following to the "Duties of Commission" entitled "Statewide Greenhouse Gas Pollution Abatement:"

> Consistent with Section 5-7-102 920(g), **the Commission shall timely promulgate implementing rules and regulations**. The implementing rules may take into account other relevant laws and rules, as ell as voluntary actions taken by local communities and the private sector, to enhance efficiency and cost-effectiveness, and shall be revised as necessary over time to ensure timely progress toward the 2025, 2030 and 2050 goals.
> CRS, § 25-7-105 (emphasis added).

Notably, in this legislation the Colorado General Assembly's complete give away of its lawmaking authority is not bounded by any specific regulatory requirements outside of the broad GHG emission reduction goals in HB 19-1261.

This reality was recently recognized by *The Colorado Sun:*[7]

> In 2019, two bills were signed by Polis, a Democrat, to address climate change. One, HB 19-1261, set goals of reducing greenhouse gas emissions by 26% over 2005 levels by 2025, 50% by 2030 and 90% by 2050. It gave the AQCC the task of

> issuing rules to meet the targets.
>
> "The challenge is: How do you make the bureaucratic machinery work as quickly as possible and get things done?" said Auden Schendler, an AQCC commissioner and Aspen Ski Co's vice president of sustainability.
>
> Some political guidance is needed on whether to make specific rules for different types of polluters, or enact statewide, economy-wide initiatives such as congestion pricing[8] to discourage people from driving or a carbon tax, Schendler said.

Governor Polis – through his newly created "Climate Cabinet" – is further directing the Colorado Department of Public Health and Environment, along with other state environmental agencies, to develop a "GHG Pollution Reduction Roadmap" to ensure "timely progress" towards the state's GHG reduction goals.[9] The Polis Administration "is currently implementing a number of bills signed into law in 2019 that will support continued progress toward GHG emission reduction targets."

Life — and the economy — in Colorado could look a lot different if the AQCC follows recommendations being developed by the Colorado Greenhouse Gas Pollution Roadmap workgroup - led by staff to the AQCC at the CDPHE. All industry, without regard to size, are in its crosshairs. So are all individual Coloradans (aka "GHG emitters")who depend on home heating and cooking using natural gas, public transportation, home and building construction, refrigerants for transport and grocery stores, and on and on. And then add state carbon "fees" on users of GHG emitting goods and services.

In *Cotrell v. City and County of Denver,* the Colorado Supreme Court noted that the test for a violation of the separation of powers required by the Colorado Constitution via an unlawful delegation of legislative authority is "not simply whether the delegation is guided by standards, but whether there are sufficient statutory standards and safeguards and administrative standards and safeguards, in combination, to protect against unnecessary and uncontrolled exercise of discretionary power."[10] This test is applied by considering whether the Legislature has properly delegated its legislative authority with "constraints [that] are sufficient to insure that administrative action will be rational and consistent in the first instance and that subsequent judicial review of that action is available and will be effective." [11] In other words, the Legislature must have put in place sufficient statutory standards or safeguards to protect from arbitrary action. HB 19-1261, with its unfettered grant of legislative authority to the AQCC based solely on meeting, "at a minimum" broad GHG reduction "goals," fails to meet this standard.

Prior delegations of emission control rulemaking authority to the AQCC, which have been upheld as lawful in Colorado, demonstrate the inadequacy of HB 19-1261. In *Lloyd A. Fry Roofing Co. v. State Dept. of Health Air Pollution Variance Board,* the Colorado Supreme Court upheld the Air Pollution Control Act of 1970 under a challenge that the Act unlawfully violated the non-delegation doctrine.[12]

The Air Pollution Control Act of 1970 delegated rulemaking authority to the predecessor of the AQCC, and directed that commission to promulgate rules for "development and maintenance of a comprehensive program for prevention, control, and abatement of air pollution throughout the entire state, including a program for control of emissions from all significant sources of air pollution, and the promulgation of ambient air goals for the state." However, that delegation was bounded by limiting the commission to promulgating regulations that take into account "various factors which either constitute, produce, or dispel air pollution, e.g., classifying different types and degrees of air pollution; promulgating regulations applicable to either a part or the whole of the state; describing maximum concentrations of contaminants that can be tolerated depending on variations in altitude, topography, climate or meteorology; taking into consideration the degree to which any particular type of emission is subject to treatment; and considering the continuous, intermittent, or seasonal nature of the emission to be controlled.[13] The Supreme Court ultimately held that these standards and safeguards on the AQCC's delegated regulatory authority were "not so broad as to result in an improper delegation of legislative authority."[14]

Unlike in *Lloyd,* HB 19-1261 does *not* have any statutory standards and safeguards governing the AQCC's future authority to promulgate enforceable regulations to achieve the legislature's GHG emission reduction goals. In *Lloyd,* the AQCC had to consider statutory factors governing types of air pollution, and standards necessary to reduce pollution levels. In HB 19-1261, the AQCC is simply given broad GHG reduction goals that are not tied to "degrees and types of air pollution," maximum concentrations of contaminants," or other factors such as geographic impacts and seasonal impacts in implementing those broad goals.[15]

While HB 19-1261 does contain some broad considerations the AQCC must incorporate into certain of its eventual regulations, those considerations are not focused on the substantive *content* of the GHG reductions, but instead on potential benefits of the regulations, such as effect on disproportionately impacted communities (HB 19-1261, Section 3; C.R.S. §25-7-105(1)(e)(III)); input from other state executive agencies lacking legislative authority (*Id.* at (1)(e)(IV); regulatory strategies employed by other jurisdictions (*Id.* at (1)(e)(V); and the costs and benefits of compliance with the eventual regulations (*Id.* at (1)(e)(VI).

The factors the AQCC was required to consider in *Lloyd* were directed at the actual rulemaking authority delegated to the commission – emission control regulations. The factors the AQCC must consider under HB 19-1261 are not related to the Commission's GHG reduction rulemaking authority, but rather to post facto justifications for those regulations. Thus under *Cotrell*, the delegation of authority under HB 19-1261 lacks sufficient standards to insure that GHG reduction regulations promulgated by the AQCC will be "rational and consistent in the first instance and that subsequent judicial review of that action is available and will be effective."[16]

As the Colorado Supreme Court noted in *Cotrell,* it is "important that individuals be protected against the unnecessary and uncontrolled exercise of this discretionary power, while still permitting a broad scope to legislative delegation where narrow legislative standards are not feasible."[17] Instead, HB 19-1261 merely creates "goals" and then gives the AQCC pure lawmaking authority – which is simply impermissible.

Conclusion

There is not a constitutional principle more essential to Colorado's democratic government than the separation of powers. The system depends on the fundamental proposition that *the Colorado General Assembly must make and be responsible for the basic policies that govern Colorado.* It is simply incompatible with that baseline necessity for a majority of the General Assembly to grant unbounded policymaking discretion to the Executive Branch.

House Bill 19-1261 does not set forth sufficient standards for the AQCC to apply promulgating GHG reduction regulations. Rather, the AQCC has essentially been given the legislature's lawmaking authority, with unfettered discretion — over the next several decades — to promulgate GHG reduction regulations without consideration any reduction *policies* set by the Colorado Legislature for achieving the broad GHG reduction goals.

The constitutional basis for permitting delegation of authority to traditional agencies was that the use of delegated power — including the power to make binding rules and authoritatively resolve adjudications — was, as a matter of constitutional power, law *execution*. Indeed, it must be, for if an agency is not engaged in law execution, it is necessarily acting unconstitutionally because the only power vested in the executive branch is the power to execute the law.[18]

Because the Colorado Constitution's basic division of powers insists that only the General Assembly can legislate, it is simply beyond the General Assembly's power to authorize any other actor actually to do so.[19]

That is the very essence of the non-delegation doctrine that the U.S. Supreme Court and other courts. Courts have always understood the line between permissible and impermissible delegations to be the line between permitting broad discretion in fulfilling the General Assembly's statutory commands (okay) and delegations providing no limit at all on that discretion (not okay). That is what the "intelligible principle" doctrinal formulation is designed to capture: whether the Executive's instructions are sufficiently knowable that they provide instructions regarding how the law is to be executed, or whether the Colorado General Assembly has given over discretion that is not subject to any limiting principle in law.

Under Colorado's Constitution, a pure delegation by the General Assembly of its lawmaking authority to the AQCC, like that set forth in HB 19-1261, is categorically out of bounds. The Colorado Constitution cares very much who exercises lawmaking authority — the legislature[20] — and how it is exercised (bicameralism and presentment)[21] — none of which bears any resemblance to the standard AQCC process of rulemaking. Rather than giving some kind of principle or standard to guide the AQCC's rules, HB 19-1261 on its face provides no standards at all, much less "intelligible" ones.

To paraphrase how the late Supreme Court Justice Antony Scalia memorably put it in a dissenting opinion in *Mistretta v. United States*, in empowering the AQCC to make standalone laws, the Colorado General Assembly had created a "sort of junior-varsity Colorado General Assembly."[22] The members of Colorado's General Assembly, constitutionally assigned to formulate policy and directly elected by the people, should be making the policy determination on whether to impose such requirements on all of Colorado's citizens — not the unelected members of the AQCC.

The passage of HB 19-1261, the Colorado General Assembly's complete give-away of its lawmaking responsibility under the Colorado Constitution, was pure malfeasance. Governor Polis signing it into law is of similar offence to Colorado's Constitution. The solution to this situation is either a successful legal challenge to the new law or a change in the legislature through the political process. Dependent on either potential remedy is education of the citizenry about what has happened and why it offends our democratic republic.

If there is a lesson in all of this it is that our Constitution is neither a self-actuating nor a self-correcting document. It requires the constant attention and devotion of all citizens. This fact is best supported by recalling the story, often told, that upon exiting Philadelphia's Constitutional Convention, Benjamin Franklin was approached by a group of citizens asking what sort of government the delegates had created. His answer was, "A republic, if you can keep it."

Benjamin Franklin's response is an American treasure, and its essential meaning is that democratic republics are not merely founded upon the consent of the people, they are also absolutely dependent upon the active and informed involvement of the people for their continued vitality.

> Paul M. Seby is a Shareholder in the Denver office of Greenberg Traurig, LLP. The views expressed in this article are solely the authors and not Greenberg Traurig, LLP.

NOTES

1. *New State Ice Co. v. Liebman*, 285 2622, 311 (1932) (Brandeis, J., dissenting)

2. Madison. *Federalist No. 51* (1788)

3. Madison. *Federalist No.* 47 (1788)

4. Jefferson. *Notes on the State of Virginia*, Query 13 (1784)

5. Colorado Constitution https://leg.colorado.gov/colorado-constitution

6. HB19-1261 Climate Action Plan To Reduce Pollution https://leg.colorado.gov/bills/hb19-1261 **and** https://leg.colorado.gov/sites/default/files/2019a_1261_signed.pdf

7. Jaffe, Mark. Colorado may have missed a deadline to plan for reducing greenhouse gasses. Now the state faces a lawsuit. Colorado Sun. July 8, 2020. (House Bill 1261) https://coloradosun.com/2020/07/08/colorado-greenhouse-gas-reduction-plan/

8. Congestion Pricing. U. S. Department of Transportation, Federal Highway Administration
https://ops.fhwa.dot.gov/congestionpricing/cp_what_is.htm

9. GHG Pollution Reduction Roadmap. Colorado Energy Office (last visited August 5, 2020).
https://energyoffice.colorado.gov/climate-energy/ghg-pollution-reduction-roadmap

10. 636 P.2d 703, 709 (Colo. 1981)

11. *Id*

12. 499 P.2d 1176 (Colo. 1972)

13. *Id.* At 1179-1180

14. *Id.* At 1180

15. *Id.* at 1180

16. *Cotrell*, 636 P.2d at 709

17. *Id.* at 708

18. U.S. CONST. art. II § 1

19. *See, e.g., Bowsher v. Synar*, 478 U.S. 714 (1986); *Immigration & Naturalization Serv. v. Chadha,* 462 U.S. 919 (1983)

20. U.S. CONST. art. I, § I

21. *Id.* § 7; *see also Immigration & Naturalization Serv. v. Chadha*, 462 U.S. 919 (1983)

22. *Id.* at 427

13

CITIZENS' VOICES OF DISSENT WILL NOT BE SILENCED: GRASSROOTS ORGANIZE TO PROTECT FUNDAMENTAL RIGHTS AND LIBERTIES

BY KIM MONSON
Radio Show Host

It is never compassionate to take others' rights, property, freedom or livelihood by the force of law, but that happened with cascading frequency in the 2020 session of the Colorado General Assembly. As a result, out of necessity, many thousands of Coloradans are becoming more actively engaged in protecting their rights by involvement in politics and policymaking. Many citizens are learning for the first time that the government does not always welcome or facilitate active citizen involvement — not even their own elected legislators.

I know this first-hand because I hear from citizens on a regular basis as a daily radio talk show host. It was disheartening during the 2019 and 2020 legislative sessions to hear individuals' disappointments and frustrations; their voices were disrespected and generally disregarded — by Politicians, Bureaucrats and "Interested Parties" currently in power at our State Capitol.

From the first day of the 2020 legislative session in January <u>to the adjournment in June, citizens watched in disbelief as</u> 46 new bills were introduced in the Senate and House after the ten week recess — on top of the $30 billion budget "Long Bill" and its record 42 "orbital bills" that would be required to actually implement the budget. For example, the raid on the accumulated millions in the Marijuana Tax Cash Fund had to be authorized by amending current law, not just inserting it in the budget to augment the General Fund.

These new, radical laws are changing the fabric of our state. The damage to our oil and gas industry, which provided jobs for tens of thousands and paid millions of dollars of taxes that support schools, libraries, roads and first responders, etc., is not only calamitous to our state's public finances, it is heart-breaking. Forced cultural changes, assault on property rights and radical educational curriculum changes are a few examples of the fundamental transformations of our economy and society engineered in 2019 and 2020 by the Democrat majorities in the House and Senate in league with our "progressive" governor.

Was there resistance to the radical legislation? Yes! Did you hear about the opposition on the major television channels' evening news programs or the Denver Post? Probably not.

Many citizens made their way to the Capitol for hearings on multiple bills, hoping their voices would be heard. Others wrote letters and/or emails and made phone calls to their representatives. They also sent messages to the governor's office. Rallies were held on the steps of the Capitol and in local communities. Meetings were held throughout the state to help educate individuals on policy, proposed laws, and powers improperly delegated to bureaucratic agencies.

Who were these individuals initiating community-based movements? They were everyday people; moms, dads, small business owners, retired military and other concerned citizens. They became grassroots activists, working on public policy issues that concerned them deeply. They weren't paid lobbyists but regular people motivated to stop terrible legislation. They were usually self-organized. They reached out and encouraged others to take action. Solid relationships and networks were built on trust, conviction and integrity — which also helps build momentum for future undertakings.

During the summer of 2019 these groups came together and succeeded in getting a veto referendum regarding the National Popular Vote on the November 2020 ballot. This referendum will ask voters whether Colorado will join the National Popular Vote Interstate Compact, which would give our state's nine Electoral College votes and our voices to the large population centers in California, New York and Illinois. The 2019 bill selling out Colorado voters to California was passed by both state chambers and signed into law by the Colorado governor. In response, regular working people across the state gathered signatures from all 64 counties to place this veto referendum on the 2020 ballot.

In November of 2019, Proposition CC was on the statewide ballot. This was an assault on the Taxpayer's Bill of Rights (TABOR). If passed it would have allowed the state to retain revenue that is now required to be refunded to taxpayers. It was defeated at the ballot box due to the tireless activity of grassroots organizations.

Unlike the professional pundit class, who were pontificating about how election year sessions are customarily more cautious and bipartisan, grassroots leaders forecasted the upcoming 2020 session to be more draconian than the previous year. Why? They expected the radical, vocal leftists who now dominate the Democrat legislative caucus would not curtail their ambitions, and that the governor would continue writing executive orders, both without much consideration for the impact on the ordinary, taxpaying citizens of the state.

During the 2019 session, HB19-1312, School Immunization Requirements, was heard in both House and Senate committees. Concerned parents and community members opposed the legislation. Over 500 people signed up to testify at committee hearings. Many mothers comforted their weary children as they waited their turn to make public comments in committee hearings. Some waited until 3:00 in the morning the next day to have their voices heard. The vast majority of people testifying were very explicit: they wanted HB 19-1312 to die. It did.

Governor Polis ignored citizen voices and sided with his bureaucrats. On June 13, 2019 Polis issued Executive Order B 2019-006, "Immediate Support for Programs and Policies to Increase State Immunization Rates." This executive edict takes away informed consent for families and students.

B 2019 006

EXECUTIVE ORDER

Immediate Support for Programs and Policies to Increase State Immunization Rates

Pursuant to the authority vested in the Governor of the State of Colorado and, in particular, pursuant to Article IV, Section 2 of the Colorado Constitution, I, Jared Polis, Governor of the State of Colorado, hereby issue this Executive Order supporting programs and policies that will increase the State's immunization rates and honor the rights of parents.

In 2019, the governor used executive orders often from August through October while the legislature was not in session. With a stroke of the pen, Governor Polis reorganized the Regional Air Quality Council to "coordinate its assessments and strategy development efforts with other air quality initiatives," including Polis' "Roadmap to 100% Renewable Energy by 2040 . . ." This frequent resort to executive orders circumvents the legislature and ignores the voices of the people. As one guest on the show stated, "The Democrat Party is now a party of elites."

Listeners who send messages to the radio show have repeatedly reminded us of a truism often lost in the dominant media's incessant buzz about renewable energy: All forms of energy are important, renewable and non-renewable, and a large majority of listeners agree with guest blogger Rick Turnquist:

> *"Whether one likes it or not, so-called fossil fuels — coal, oil, natural gas and natural gas liquids— power and promote the advanced modern civilization we now enjoy. Electricity, which gives us everything from air conditioning to high definition TVs to the smart phones progressives use to attack fossil fuels, is mostly generated by coal. Thanks to clean coal technologies and*

> *carbon capture, power generation from coal is cleaner than ever. Oil powers our transportation. From our private cars to airliners to giant cargo ships, oil is what makes them go . . Natural gas is used for electricity generation and is what keeps most of our homes warm in the winter".*[1]

On opening day in January of 2020, legislators were met on the West Steps of the Capitol with a rally sponsored by a grassroots group, Stand for Colorado. This rally resulted from multiple phone calls from listeners on the show who wanted to replicate the rally held at the end of the 2019 legislative session. Repeatedly, the comment was, "We want the legislators to know that we are present and watching. We haven't forgotten what you did last year."

A collective group of speakers spoke that January morning on Second Amendment rights, healthcare, paid family leave, vaccinations, financial transparency, and educational freedom, to name a few topics. The energy exhibited at the rally was sustained throughout the session by grassroots activists. Will people be free to act in accordance with their unalienable rights of life, liberty and the pursuit of happiness, or will the radical left agenda of complete control over the lives of people become the new norm in Colorado — or the "New Normal," as the state's governor likes to call it?

Within the first few days in January we got our answer. The continued assault on individual freedom and property rights would continue, and at a heightened level, with 164 bills introduced the first week alone. As a result, more people began paying attention to the new legislative session and revisited the consequences of previous bills.

In the first week alone, from opening day on January 8 to the following Tuesday the 14th, 212 bills were introduced, and in the blink of an eye, over 270 new bills were being discussed within the Capitol. A pattern was very evident. Any important bill sponsored and favored by Republican members was usually sent to the "kill" committee if the bill lacked a Democrat co-sponsor. Although it was disturbing, grassroots activists did not relinquish their voices and continued to send emails/letters and call representatives at the Capitol and the governor's office.

Listener/guest Allen Thomas recently observed:

> *On and on the record of government force plays on. But I don't see that record playing and creating the scenes I have seen the past few weeks. I don't see the government efficiently helping the lives of others. We need to be the change we wish to see in the world, and not ask the government to be that change. Because we have seen that the media and the government can obfuscate and confuse, but neighbors can actually make a difference, even if it is simply one roll of two-ply at a time.* [2]

At the end of January, students from Colorado Christian University in Lakewood attended the March for Life rally in Washington, D.C. The enthusiasm of the students and adults was vivid as they carried flags directly behind the front banner. The value of human life was validated by thousands of people of all ages, ethnicity and religions. One way that brought that message home in Colorado was Initiative 120, "*Due Date Too Late.*"

If adopted by a vote of the people in November of 2020, the Initiative — which will appear as Proposition 115 on the November ballot — will prohibit abortions in Colorado after a fetus reaches 22 weeks, which science shows is when the baby feels pain.

The Initiative effort was in the middle of its petition drive when the session started in January. As Giuliana Day, a primary sponsor of the initiative stated, one of the "dark secrets in this state" is that an abortion can be performed for any reason up until birth with no restrictions. The Initiative needed to collect nearly 125,000 valid signatures by March 1 in order to appear on the November ballot. It was strictly a grassroots effort with an all-volunteer staff. Signatures were turned in and on March 18 it was announced by the Secretary of State's office that a complete count of signatures needed to be performed. On April 3 the office stated that only 114,647 signatures were valid and that an additional 9,985 valid signatures were needed to qualify for the November ballot. Fortunately, the grassroots activists had already sued the Colorado Secretary of State's office to extend the 15-day cure period due to the coronavirus and stay-at-home orders. The Denver District Court judge granted an emergency stay which allowed *Due Date Too Late* to collect the needed additional signatures.

Volunteers resumed signature collection on May 15 and were successful in obtaining more than the required 9,985 valid signatures. On June 8 the office stated that an additional 38,557 valid signatures were obtained during the curing process for a total of 153,204 valid signatures. That meant that 120 — now Proposition 115 — had indeed qualified for the November3 ballot.

The tremendous grassroots effort to qualify a pro-life ballot measure illustrates the resolve of multitudes of citizens to not be ignored by the radical elites now in control of state government in Colorado. When year after year pro-life bills are routinely sent to kill committees, citizens organized to have their voices heard — at the ballot box.

We have seen such grassroots activism often when frustrated business organizations resort to petition campaigns to place corrective measures on the ballot. In 2020, a coalition of organizations collected nearly 200,000 signatures to place a proposition on the ballot to limit the government's power to use increased fees to fund government programs when voters may not approve additional taxes. As water runs downhill, citizens will put up with only so much government arrogance before taking their grievance directly to the ballot box.

As the end of January approached, 288 bills were listed on the Colorado legislative website. Bills for life, liberty and the pursuit of happiness were thrown to the kill committees, while the radical leftist agenda bills were advancing. The radical leftist agenda was palpable.

At the beginning of February 2020, there was an announcement that the public was invited to testify at a Joint Budget Committee (JBC) meeting to voice what individuals thought the priorities should be for the next budget. It sounded inviting; however, it was for one day, or should we say, one afternoon, as the time was set for 1:30-5pm. It is highly inconvenient for everyday, hardworking people to attend a week-day afternoon hearing, particularly with little notice.

There are many barriers for citizens to make public comment at Capitol committee hearings. One is time; many people work and are not able to take time off. Also, many people live miles and hours away from the Capitol and cannot justify the trip for a 2-3 minute comment. During this age of internet communication, it is hard to believe there is not a technology option for all citizens to attend or at least view committee hearings. As expected, the majority of witnesses at the afternoon committee hearing were lobbyists and spokespersons for organized interest groups, not ordinary citizens paying taxes.

In mid- February the grassroots activists received a slap in the face. The vaccination bill that was defeated in 2019 came back to life.

The new bill, SB20-163, School Entry Immunization, took even more control away from parents and their right to choose for their children. Remember, this follows on the heels of Governor Polis' executive order signed in June 2019. The pharmaceutical industry was again backing the legislation which again set up a furious debate. One of the key stipulations of the new bill was that parents are required to take an online "re-education" class via the internet distributed by the health department or receive a medical exemption "certificate" from a doctor in order to exempt a child from a vaccination. Regardless of which route is taken, the information will be maintained in the state's immunization registry. Like last year, about five hundred parents with children in-hand showed up and a few were allowed to testify before the Senate hearing. Once again, the leftist politicians disregarded the personal stories and appeals from citizens, and the bill passed the committee on a party-line vote.

Lawmaking at the Capitol was suspended in both chambers on March 14th due to the COVID-19/Wuhan Virus, and did not reconvene for business until ten weeks later, on May 26th. The Joint Budget Committee's (JBC's) job during the recess was to reduce the current year and FY2021 budgets by about $3.3 billion due to the predicted loss of sales and income tax revenue. Most constituents believed — based on statements by Democrat leaders — that the budget bill and accompanying School Finance bill would consume most of the work of the extended session after the lawmakers returned. Unbeknownst to citizens, that was not the real agenda.

Favored bills of the Democrat majority were once again front and center, including the vaccination bill. To supposedly expedite proceedings and finish all necessary legislative business by the end of June, multiple restrictions were placed on committee hearings and public witnesses. To limit exposure to COVID-19, all Capitol visitors, including employees, had their temperatures checked daily upon entering the building by a volunteer group, and individuals were asked a series of questions. If they were deemed to not be "healthy" they were asked to leave. If allowed to enter, they received a wrist band to be worn at all times while in the Capitol. And, of course, they were required to wear a mandatory mask.

Citizens monitored the activity at the Capitol on a daily, if not hourly, basis. Conflicting reports of budget cuts and bills to be heard in committee were continuous. The confusion for the grassroots community was high. The vaccination bill garnered uninterrupted attention and was closely tracked.

On Friday, June 5, the end of the second week of the renewed session, the *Colorado Sun* reported: [3]

"We were told that everything is going to be 'fast, friendly and free,'" said House Minority Leader Patrick Neville, R-Castle Rock, quoting remarks from House Speaker KC Becker about what policies Democrats would push through during the abbreviated legislative term. "They basically have gotten rid of the 'friendly and free' concept. We're going to finish that up and get rid of the 'fast' concept."

The efforts to hold up legislating came after Democrats announced that the vaccine measure, Senate Bill 163, would receive a hearing Sunday in a House committee.

Representative Neville's comments were reflective of the community's sentiments. An important hearing on less than 72 hours' notice — and on a Sunday no less! To push this bill through, the committee set additional rules: the hearing would convene for only 90 minutes with each side receiving 45 minutes for comment, and each person speaking would only be allowed 2 minutes, not the usually allotted time of 3 minutes.

With a very tight schedule, activists were mobilized. A rally was scheduled on the east steps of the Capitol Sunday morning before the hearing. Multiple hundreds of activists were present despite the protesters on the west steps, some who came to the east side and were disruptive and disrespectful to those peacefully assembling. Robert F. Kennedy, Jr. flew in to be the main speaker. He also testified at the hearing against the vaccination bill.

Hearing SB-163 Social distancing guidelines enforced

In the
committee hearing, the majority party committee members were rude, arrogant, and in the end, totally disregarded the valid concerns voiced by citizens. Instead, the committee

passed a bill heavily sponsored and lobbied by the pharmaceutical industry. The bill passed the Senate and House and was signed by the governor.

The 72nd General Assembly could not end soon enough with the barrage of horrendous bills. The legislators consistently ignored citizens' voices. Many times legislators made it extremely difficult for citizen's voices to be heard in committees, especially after the legislators reconvened after the suspension. Many grass roots activists believed the best thing that came out of the session was that it was 36 days short of the usual 120 due to COVID-19.

Throughout 2020, grassroots activists worked at the local government level as well. The coronavirus brought out the worst in local governments and bureaucracies of the various county health departments.

On June 3, Andrew Roise, founder of Reopen Colorado, was a guest on The Kim Monson Show. Roise reflected on the events of Sunday, April 19, when he led a large rally at the State Capitol where thousands demanded that the governor reopen Colorado. Within the same week Governor Polis did state that he would begin to loosen restrictions on people and businesses. Yet, that statement proved to be misleading as people were still restricted in their movements and many businesses were highly constrained in activity or closed months later. Roise stated that the COVID-19/Wuhan Virus reaction by the political establishment is not driven by objective science but by politics.

Bureaucratic institutions are powerful and there are few tools to hold them accountable. State and county health departments are prime examples. The chain of public trust is broken, as health departments are influenced by the billions of dollars spent to frame and influence policy.

One business that experienced the iron hand of a health department enforcement is the owner of Waters Edge Winery in Arapahoe County, Jennifer Hulan. On May 5, 2020, as she was preparing for afternoon patrons to arrive, Hulan received a warning from the Tri-County Health Department that began:

> **WARNING**
> YOU ARE HEREBY INFORMED OF
> POTENTIAL LEGAL ACTIONS
> WHICH MAY BE TAKEN AGAINST YOU FOR
> FAILURE TO COMPLY WITH ORDER ISSUED
> BY THE COLORADO DEPARTMENT OF
> PUBLIC HEALTH AND ENVIRONMENT.

Warning, legal actions, comply and order are all threatening words: county government officials will hurt you if you do not obey. Hulan's business was temporarily forced to close by the Tri-County Health Department while some businesses were blessed with the arbitrary term "essential business" and allowed to remain open. Elected county officials, thrilled with this new power, hid behind health department boards and bureaucrats. From the governor we soon saw a flurry of over 100 Executive Orders, plus new rules, regulations and enforcement actions from city councils, mayors, and county commissioners.

During the initial mask mandating in Colorado in March, the mayor of Lone Tree opined, in an emergency virtual city council meeting, that it is a "privilege" for our businesses to open. In the words of our nation's Declaration of Independence, individuals have a God given right to "Life, Liberty and the Pursuit of Happiness." But apparently no longer, not in 2020. We must now ask our new overlords in state government and public health departments if we can speak, move, assemble, worship, and work.

There are many more bills, executive orders and local rules and regulations that I've not addressed but have greatly affected the citizens of Colorado. Grassroots activists, loosely formed or highly structured, continue to work to preserve our freedoms.

My friends and fellow citizens, we are moving toward a tyrannical state, where neighbors snitch on neighbors, where we must have permission to move about and work, where we are forbidden from going to Church to worship. This is madness.

It is time to engage energetically in this Battle of Ideas raging in American today. Put on your thinking caps. Ask, what, why, when, how, where and who? Engage in thoughtful and reasonable conversations with friends, family and colleagues. Write personal notes and call your city council members, mayors, county commissioners, state senators and representatives, the governor and health department bureaucrats.

> *"The only thing necessary for the triumph of evil is for good men to do nothing."* Edmund Burke

NOTES

1. Monson, Kim. *Energy and Mobility: The Democrat War on Modern Life.* The Kim Monson Show. February 26, 2020

2. Monson, Kim. *The Good of the Neighbor is Greater than the Good of the Government.* The Kim Monson Show. April 17, 2020

3. Paul, Jesse and Brown, Jennifer. *Republicans stopped Colorado's vaccine bill last year with delay tactics. Will they work again?* The Colorado Sun. June 5, 2020 https://coloradosun.com/2020/06/05/colorado-vaccine-bill-republican-delay-tactics/

14

ACTIVIST MEDIA PROTECT THE MOB: THE ARROGANCE OF THE CORRUPT COORDINATED DEMOCRAT MEDIA MACHINE

BY RANDY CORPORON
Attorney and Political Activist

Edgar Allen Poe died in 1849 at age forty, just four days after he was found deliriously wandering the streets of Baltimore. Five years before his untimely and unexplained death, Poe wrote of a traveler vacationing in southern France in the Fall of 1844. This unnamed traveler thought the opportunity to visit "too good to be lost" as he passed near a "Maison de Sante," one of France's infamous insane asylums, or, as the traveler translated to English, "a private mad-house."

In his essay describing the experience, *The System of Dr. Tarr and Professor Fether,*[1] Poe's unnamed traveler is shocked to learn of a recent, severe change in the operation of this Maison de Sante. Their uniquely original practices such as no punishments of any kind and rare confinements, which had spread throughout the country's private asylums to tremendous acclaim, had been eliminated. The superintendent, Monsieur Maillard, had returned to traditional "treatment" methods, which included physical punishment, restraints, separation and confinement. The traveler, who had heard through his "medical friends" in Paris that this "system of soothing" was universally adopted throughout the country, told Maillard, "I am very much surprised at what you tell me; for I have made sure that, at this moment, no other method of treatment for mania existed in any part of the country." Maillard replied, "You are young yet, my friend, but the time will arrive when you learn to judge for yourself of what is going on in the world, without trusting to the gossip of others. *Believe nothing you hear and only one-half that you see."*

When it comes to Colorado's mass-media machine, that advice is, hands-down, a no-brainer!

My research to find the origin of the quote "the inmates have taken over the asylum" led me back only as far as the 1920's. Though Poe never uses the phrase in that 1845 story, which is built around that premise, I could find no earlier examples of the concept. If you substitute "win-at-all-cost radical leftists" for "inmates," and you believe that left-wing government and its supportive mass-media machine are the inmates' modern asylum, as I do, then you will understand my point below. In other words, "if the shoe fits, wear it."

In Colorado in 2020, intelligent observers already know the inmates have indeed taken over the asylum. The radical left primarily controls the reins of governmental power and does so in partnership with the state's mass media machine.

In March 2020, Democrat Governor Jared Polis seized legislatively designed (and the lawyer in me argues, unconstitutionally created) “emergency” powers under the 1984 Colorado Disaster Relief Act. He acted in response to a dangerous and, at the time, largely unknown disease, a “coronavirus” which had originated in Wuhan, China.

As an aside, according to the mass-media machine, this disease can only be called COVID-19 lest you, I, and especially the President of the United States, be deemed a racist for reminding anyone of its undisputed origins in China. This stricture is rigorously enforced despite the fact that, in January, news outlets considered mainstream, such as MSNBC, CNN, NBC, NPR, *Bloomberg, New York Times, Los Angeles Times, Washington Post* and, yes, Colorado's *Denver Post*, all referred to the Chinese and/or Wuhan Virus countless times.

Use of such location references was common in all media up to and during January 2020 until Democrats seized the virus’ name as another "blame-it-on-Trump" campaign issue. All these news outlets now decree that, during the run-up to the re-election effort of Donald J. Trump, use of words such as Chinese, Communist Party, Wuhan, grouped together or individually and added to the word virus, indicate (no, conclusively prove!) that the speaker is a racist. Nonetheless, I call it the Chinese, Communist Party, Wuhan Virus in order to remind people, not that the good people of China are responsible for unleashing it on the world, but that their Communist Party rulers are.

In responding to the Wuhan Virus pandemic declared by the federal Centers for Disease Control, Governor Polis used his self-determined emergency powers to decide which Colorado businesses were "essential," such as marijuana dispensaries and abortion clinics, and which ones were not and, thus, could be ordered closed. By August, the Governor has unilaterally extended these "emergency powers" for over five months with no end in sight. He has expanded these powers from closing or restricting businesses and ordering people to stay home, with certain exceptions, to ordering people, including children eleven years old and up, to cover the lower half of their faces in public, decreeing that bars that don't serve food must shut down, and mandating that restaurants who serve alcohol cut off adult beverage service at 10:00 pm (then a month later, 11:00 pm) — and damn well be able to prove it should government inspectors or armed liquor enforcement agents decide to inquire. Apparently, even as the Wuhan virus gets older, it's not able to stay out later. But you are. Your King has decreed it.

Under the Disaster Emergency Relief Act, the Democrat-majority state legislature could, with or without a few votes from the Republican minority, pass a joint resolution by majority vote to end the Polis emergency declaration. Under the Act, the Polis emergency declaration was to last only 30 days. However, without a joint resolution from the legislature or a successful court challenge (currently, the seven-member Colorado Supreme Court is made up of six Democrats and only one Republican appointee), Governor Polis can extend his unilateral decision-making every 30 days, *indefinitely*. (Note: Some legislative Resolutions require a two-thirds "super-majority" vote, but in the case of the statute giving the Governor special emergency powers, only a simple majority is required. Not too surprisingly, the Democrat majority in the Colorado General Assembly has thus far declined to exercise that option).

As we will explore below, and admittedly with occasional exceptions, in the Queen City of the Plains, the television media I grew up with along with our only remaining "major" newspaper, the *Denver Post*, are content to, using the Chinese Communist Party Wuhan Virus name "restrictions" as just one example, primarily toe the Democrat Party line. Every day from April to August was filled with reports of the number of "cases." Minimal analysis, or even straight-up reporting, was offered regarding *favorable* trends, such as a *declining rates* of new cases, hospitalizations and deaths. Why isn't it front page or TV/radio headline news that, according to the Colorado Department of Health and Environment (CDPHE);[2] as of August 28, 2020, over five full months into the pandemic:

- Almost 90% of the coronavirus-related deaths in Colorado are people age 60 and over, even though the 60 and over age-group comprises only 20% of Colorado's population and 19% of the cases?
- That 53% of deaths are age 80 and over, even though that age group is only 3% of the population and fewer than 5% of the Virus cases?
- That the millions of Coloradans under age 40 have experienced less than 1.6% of the virus-related deaths?
- That institutional living (nursing homes, assisted-living centers) is the riskiest, most dangerous environment for contracting and dying from the disease?
- Why is there not a news focus on the fact that Colorado has abundant, available medical treatment options?
- That the $66,000-per-day cost of the *never used,* Polis-decreed "Colorado Convention Center emergency hospital" has now been shrunken from 2000 beds to 250?

And so much more. Why no in-depth coverage of the horrific social and economic consequences of the Governor's five-months-and-counting "emergency orders," which are destroying our state's economic and social fabric every single day?

I'm not talking about the political fights over extended unemployment, initial food shortages in food banks, and the Left's insatiable need for more social spending. I'm talking about front-page or newscast leading stories about the ongoing destruction of Colorado families' life-long dreams.

In a rare exception to the focus on case numbers, on August 11, 2020, the *Denver Post* reported on the front page that, according to the Colorado Restaurant Association, 62% of the restaurants in Colorado will close forever within six months under current or worsening conditions. Many are already gone (Morton's Steakhouse downtown, The Fresh Fish Company after over four decades, C&C Coffee Kitchen in Castle Rock to name a few) and other small businesses are seeing similar disasters.

These and other predictable and preventable social and economic consequences do not arise from the fact that we're dealing with a novel virus, one which is primarily dangerous to elderly, ill, and confined persons. The virus did not cause these severe dislocations and human tragedies. They arise from the Governor and his health experts' exercise of and preference for unilateral control, their tunnel-vision focus on numbers of cases factored into ineffective, inaccurate, and sometimes non-existent modeling. And, in the opinion of many, the Governor's actions stem from a clear understanding that if life returns to normal and the economy begins to hum too soon — that is, before November 3 —

Democrats will pay the price on election day.

It is undeniable that the current and worsening economic conditions referred to by the *Post* are being caused by government actions, not by the health impact of the Wuhan Virus. Outside of a few conservative talk radio stations, web sites, small newspapers, and news aggregators in Colorado, there is no focused reporting or analysis of these other critical, and one might say opposing, trends and factors by the major print and electronic media.

Using the definitions of the terms I laid out above, it is clear that the inmates have taken over the asylum. As a result, *believe nothing that you hear and only one-half that you see.*

We did not arrive at this precipice by accident.

This book is titled, *UNMASKED2020: Colorado's Radical Left Turn and a Warning to America*. Anyone who's uncertain of the brilliant, simple strategy that brought Colorado to this place, and hasn't already done so, should also read a book published a decade ago in 2010, *The Blueprint, How Democrats Won Colorado and Why Republicans Everywhere Should Care*, by Adam Schrager and Rob Witwer.[3] It is the story of the planned takeover of Colorado state government by a group of four multimillionaires who began coordinating their political funding and endorsements, and their financial support for a network of progressive non-profit organizations, way back in 2004. One of those four innovative kingmakers was Colorado's current Governor, Jared Polis.

Over the past two decades, Conservatives and Republicans have been out-planned, out-played, and out-spent by people who are now permitting and, in many cases, embracing an effort to win a presidential election through orchestrated chaos.

Who profits most from the planned downsizing of the dynamic growing economy Colorado and the nation were enjoying at the end of February2020? Before our Governor let "health experts" take over managing our economy, did we see such chaos, pessimism and desperation? Before the Governor assumed nearly unlimited emergency powers on March 11, 2020, and set our economy on "self-destruct," did we see Marxist-run mobs attacking police officers, citizens and the State Capitol, anarchy in our streets, cancel culture, and paradoxically, virtually limitless government power, all supported by the most activist, corrupt, coordinated media myth-making machine in history?

21st Century technology makes such coordination easier now than at any time in history. Once the desired messages for the news cycle, or the election cycle, are selected, variations of the same themes can be produced in a matter of minutes and shared with hundreds of thousands, even millions, of people in a matter of seconds. Multiple independent assessments of story choices from hour-to-hour and, day-to-day news story logs, make unassailable the fact that the most well-known TV and print media outlets lean to the left. From the conservative Media Research Center, through articles in non-media focused publications like *Investor's Business Daily*, to liberal sites like *Huffington Post*, or even the self-proclaimed unbiased, balanced news site, AllSides[4] all acknowledge that the television and print outlets I have identified above are Progressive-Left or Radical Left in their reporting. Newspapers and television news departments are entitled to have strong opinions and political biases; it is the uniformity and echo-chamber effects of this uniform Leftist bias that is subversive to the goal of a well-informed public.

Talk radio remains the single, strongest opposition to leftist media dominance. The most successful conservative outlets and effective shows make quite clear that they are presenting opinions, not masking their opinions under a claim of neutral observation or simple presentation of facts.

As demonstrated by the massive collapse in 2010 of *Air America*, the largest commercial effort that tried to compete in the talk radio marketplace from the Left, Liberal radio just doesn't cut it on its own. Left-wing *NPR Radio* has managed to survive, but only at taxpayer expense.

So, what shall we call this focused, effective, disastrous media machine? In a 2012 article[5] columnist Mike Paranzino identified and dismissed several options. "Mainstream media" or the "MSM" isn't accurate. He pointed out that pornography is far more popular than NBC or the *New York Times*, but that doesn't make it mainstream.

In a 2019 Gallup poll,[6] only 26% of Americans polled identified themselves as liberal, with 35% conservative and 35% moderate. In other words, by almost 3-1, the liberal view is still the minority view in America. But, because Liberals control entertainment, media and, sadly, so much of the education system, they convince themselves that they hold the popular view, use their platforms to persuade people who aren't dialed into the same, and work overtime to dishearten conservatives into believing that we are out of touch with real America, "their" America. It's a tactic, an effective one, and one we must overcome at election time and beyond.

How about Drive By Media or State Run Media, Rush Limbaugh's favorite designations for the liberal media machine? I have to admit, I chuckle when I hear them, but I don't really know what Drive By Media means and, when Republicans are in charge, State Run Media doesn't really apply.

Denver talk radio legend Mike Rosen, who always made it a point to tell you where he sat before he told you where he stood, referred to "them" as the Dominant Liberal Media, as I recall, and was always quick to remind us that public regard for this predominantly lefty media was at historic lows. It still is, as local liberal news stations, especially on TV, compete for a piece of an ever-shrinking pie and the more conservative cable TV channel, Fox News, continues to dominate programming with often as many as nine out of ten of the top-rated shows in the Neilson ratings.

Newt Gingrich has favored the term, Elite Media, which I guess can create some disdain in the everyday person, the working *schmo* (or *schmo-ette*) who feels controlled or snubbed by those "betters." While each of those names have one form of appeal or another, none of them pack the punch that's required. We need a name that reminds us, especially now in the midst of lefty media's, round-the-clock Trump Derangement Syndrome during the run-up to the November election, just how much bias "they" bring and, potentially, how much damage "they" can do. We have the tools at hand to understand, confront, and expose them such as talk radio, instant access online to information, video, alternative opinions and more, and social media for sharing if we're willing to do the work. But, often, time is short and something pithy can make the difference. If you have ideas, I hope you will send them to me.[7]

In the meantime, I'm going with the Corrupt Coordinated Democrat Media Machine. Not short enough to be pithy, perhaps. But, again, if the shoe fits . . .

Have we always been prey to a Corrupt, Coordinated, Democrat Media Machine in Colorado? No, in fact, it is a fairly recent arrival. As a Denver native born in 1959, it was the norm growing up for our *Rocky Mountain News* to be delivered in the morning and the *Denver Post* to be delivered in the afternoon. I knew nothing then about Republican versus Democrat political viewpoints, conservative versus liberal perspectives, editorial license, or competition for the news consumers' dollars. I thought that a morning paper explained what happened the night before and an afternoon paper described what happened earlier that day. It wasn't until much later in life that I learned that the *Rocky Mountain News* was started in 1859 as a weekly broadsheet (the same newspaper style as the *Denver Post*), was Colorado's oldest newspaper and perhaps Colorado's longest running business, and that the co-publisher of the first edition was a woman who accompanied the printing press as it rode on an oxcart from Omaha, Nebraska to the part of the Kansas Territory that would eventually include Denver.

I had no idea, then, that the *Denver Post*, self-described "Voice of the Rocky Mountain Empire," was originally the *Evening Post* starting in 1892, then the *Denver Evening Post*. It was actually founded to stem the departure of Colorado Democrats from the Democrat Party over the presidential nomination of Grover Cleveland (because Cleveland disfavored the Federal Government's purchase of a critical and profitable Colorado asset: silver). Go figure!

The only distinctions I really drew at the time, as a comic strip connoisseur and "paper boy" delivering the afternoon *Post* from the huge canvas bags hanging from the front of my bicycle, were that that the *Rocky's* eventual tabloid style was much easier to manage than the *Post's* broadsheet design and that Sundays seemed to be a competition to see which paper weighed the most. But, as the inability of the news market to support two newspapers inexorably led to the demise of the *Rocky Mountain News*, the paper always considered the more conservative of the two, the distinctions in perspective became much clearer.

Eventually, in 2001, the two newspapers tried combining resources with both producing a daily paper during the week and, for the weekend, the *Rocky* only publishing on Saturday and the *Post* only publishing on Sunday. They each provided a single page of editorial content for the other for their weekend versions. The two editorial staffs had a healthy battle of ideas each weekend and the political leanings of each became much clearer. When the two daily, one-weekend model failed, the last *Rocky* printed on February 27, 2009, and only the *Denver Post* was left standing. The speaker of the Colorado State House at the time, Democrat Terrence D. Carroll said, "I'm afraid of the echo chambers that are emerging because more people are choosing to get their news only from sources that reinforce what they want to believe." [8]

The *Denver Post* did, and still does to some small extent, provide a forum for some conservative perspectives on its opinion pages. However, what is tolerated as permissible speech and presentable ideas is wildly divergent depending on where within the political spectrum one resides. It is perfectly acceptable in the editorial section of the *Post* for lefties to justify, if not celebrate, the defacing and destruction of historic buildings and statues or the burning of cities in the name of social justice and the "right" to rip perfectly healthy human babies from the womb of their mothers right up until the time of their birth. But, a conservative columnist, Jon Caldara, who dares to express the simple and scientifically unassailable idea that there are but two biological genders, male and female, can — and did! — find himself relieved of his role as a rare voice of opposition to the leftist drumbeat.

Outright falsehoods, like the claim that President Trump supports white supremacists because he said there were good people on both sides of an event in Charlottesville where a young woman was killed by a supremacist, are repeated so often that they become part of subsequent stories and are treated as fact. President Trump was referring to people arguing for and against the removal of historic statues, not to people engaged in violence, and he expressly and emphatically said so.[9]

A reporter recently provided what was presented as news coverage in the *Denver Post* of a July 19, 2020, Pro Police Rally in Denver's Civic Center Park, where Denver police were ordered to stand by and not interfere as domestic terrorists, who announced their intentions publicly several days prior in a "Stop the Pig Rally" posting, caused property damage and physical injury to participants. They prevented police supporters from even completing the Pledge of Allegiance and one patriotic song. I was the emcee for this rally. The reporter called me and quoted me accurately. But, in the title to the story, the reporter described the patriotic event and the criminal attack as "dueling rallies." When I personally told her that describing the attack this way was outrageous, her only response was that "(a) story commentator also raised that objection. Thanks for the feedback." But the misleading reference was never changed.

As a full-time conservative political activist and part-time talk radio host, I am probably more focused than most on shadowy story manipulations, intentional or otherwise, that occur in news reports every single day. Often, those of us who still use radios flip through our favorite stations, especially at commercial breaks, but may stick around after a good tease about an upcoming guest, story, or news headline.

A hot topic for conservatives this election season is voter fraud. One single word can completely spin a "news" story about a Tweet or comment by President Trump. For example, on July 30, 2020, President Trump tweeted: "With Universal Mail-In Voting (not Absentee Voting, which is good), 2020 will be the most INACCURATE & FRAUDULENT Election in history. It will be a great embarrassment to the USA. Delay the Election until people can properly, securely and safely vote?" Provocative? Sure. Stimulative of strong *opinions* across the political spectrum? Certainly, and I would say intentionally so. The Left says there is no evidence of significant voter fraud. Yet, to those on the right, voter fraud is well-documented in, for example, a non-exhaustive study by The Heritage Foundation. This single analysis identifies almost 1300 cases of voter fraud which resulted in nearly 1200 criminal and/or civil penalties[10] including some in Colorado.

The Democrat push for all-mail balloting systems to be set-up in all states as a response to the COVID-19 virus and an increased understanding on the right of strategies such as ballot harvesting[11] and endless recounts to a desired outcome[12] create a reasonable basis for skepticism, inquiry and debate.

A news report on the President's Tweet could fairly say, "Today in a Tweet, for the first time President Trump posed the question about whether this November's election should be delayed as a result of voter fraud." Yet, in countless stories, including television, print, or network feeds and local reads by radio news reporters, the "reporting" was: "Today in a Tweet, for the first time President Trump posed the question about whether this November's election should be delayed as a result of *unsubstantiated allegations* of voter fraud[emphasis added]." On August 25, 2002, in an *AP* story printed on the front page of the *Denver Post* about President Trump's concerns around election integrity, the author refers to Trump's "unsupported concerns."

That happens so frequently, so casually, that we barely notice it. The honest news reporters and, especially, the casual viewers and listeners, don't begin to understand just how much we are being played by the tiny number of companies (6) that control the vast majority of the mainstream news today[13] and have for some time.[14]

There is a relatively new online news and opinion source in Colorado that I have had great hope for. It's called the *Colorado Sun* and it has an opportunity to be a provider of significant original content rather than reprinting so much copy from liberal sources such as the *New York Times*, the *Washington Post, AP,* etc. as the *Denver Post*, with a skeleton crew, is forced to do.(Don't get me wrong. The *Post* is forced to use stories from other sources, NOT to insure they come from the same *highly partisan* sources).

In a very timely piece for me as I finish writing this chapter, on August 25 the Sun did a story entitled "How Colorado Republicans Transformed from Never-Trump to Trump Loyalists in Four Years."[15]

As one of the state's Ted Cruz delegates to the 2016 Republican National Convention who opposed Donald Trump, I don't care that I wasn't interviewed for the piece. Those that were interviewed expressed their current positions well. But, with only one exception among the interviewees, none of us were actually "Never-Trump." I always described myself at the time as "Barely Trump" once Trump became the nominee. As the article helped explain, Donald Trump was an unknown quantity for conservatives prior to his election, so many of our votes were cast in opposition to Hillary Clinton. President Trump has delivered on so much of his promised conservative agenda that he has won a vast majority of us over.

The nuances between the different 2016 delegates, such as Never-Trump versus Barely-Trump, may not have been significant to the interviewees or the author of the piece. But it is fascinating to note that, in the daily newsletter that goes out in an effort to draw attention to their stories from the day before, *The Sunriser*, following a teaser paragraph from and a link to the Trump loyalist story, has 4 bullet-point references to other "related" stories:

1) "This year's attendees to the RNC from Colorado say the limited in-person event has been "spectacular," a story from their publication. (OK.);

2) "Night 2 of the convention was "another tsunami of untruths" from the president and other speakers, according to fact-checker" from the *Washington Post*. (Oh, really?);

3) "The Trump administration is also under fire for using the powers and assets of the federal government as props for a political campaign — a form of corruption that could be a violation of the Hatch Act" from, you guessed it, the *Washington Post*. (Is there a pattern developing here?); and

4) "The RNC pulled a speaker after she tweeted an

anti-Semitic rant yesterday [emphasis added], but still featured a speaker who said it would be "smart" of police to racially profile her adopted "brown son" and endorsed a "household voting" system that would take votes away from wives," from *Politico* and the *Huffington Post*. (Am I "paranoid" if someone really is following me?).

How do you explain phrases like "dueling rallies" and "unsubstantiated" or "unsupported allegations" in a "news" story, and story groupings like the one I just described, without concluding that the bias runs deep in those organizations?

I am told by people who have studied the history of journalism in America, and a brief review confirms, that partisan newspapers are nothing new. But their partisanship was clear for all to see. They didn't pretend to be what they are not, balanced. The new thing that allows them to get away with it now is lack of competition. Throughout the latter 19th century and well into the 20th, most large cities, not unlike Denver, had dueling Republican and Democrat newspapers. Well into the late 20th century, Sacramento had the Democrat *Sacramento Bee* and the Republican *Sacramento Union*. Washington, DC had both the *Post* and the more Republican *Washington Star* well into the '60s. Phoenix had the more Democrat-leaning *Phoenix Gazette* before the *Arizona Republic* became the sole source of newsprint. But today, in most large cities, few such competing voices have survived.

As further evidence that you should *believe nothing you hear and only one-half that you see*, I will leave you with an example from a popular local television figure.

Kyle Clark is a news anchor on the NBC affiliate in Denver,

Channel 9, KUSA, and the host of *Next* with Kyle Clark. *Next* is described on its *Facebook* page as "like the news . . . only new." At times, Clark provides commentary, which is clearly defined as such, and he is active on social media. Of course, these are both appropriate venues for presenting his opinions, causes, ideas. His Twitter feed is a good place to ascertain where he stands politically (as is mine and, hopefully, as is yours if you have one).

A meeting I recently had with Mike Lindell, the recovering methamphetamine addict, profoundly successful creator of the *My Pillow* line of bed and bath products, and a strong supporter of President Trump, got me thinking about a prime example from Clark which exposes his smug, elitist views. When Lindell decided to devote his production facilities to making personal protection equipment during the height of the Chinese Communist Party Wuhan Virus, television networks covered the press conference announcement. Lindell, who attributes his drug sobriety to welcoming God into his life, encouraged people to read the Bible during his remarks[16].

In response, on March 30, 2020, Clark tweeted: "TV Networks are airing a My Pillow commercial. Ok" followed by "The pillow guy is explaining how America must turn back to God and praising the President." The disdain drips from the post, and many of Clark's Twitter followers picked up on it, even called him on it.

For people of faith, Lindell's remarks were affirming and reassuring, a reminder of a higher power that promises a better day and the opportunity in America, greater than anywhere else in the world, to create our own rags-to-riches tales. For non-believers, at the least, the remarks were quaint, rendered with kindness, and without condemnation.

This is but one example, but the derision flowing from the simple tweet exemplifies how elite know-it-alls, like Clark, view those of us who see Lindell as a fallen, now inspiring, American, God-praising success story.

Kyle Clark @KyleClark · Mar 30
The pillow guy is explaining how America must turn back to God and praising the President.
67 23 124

Perhaps Clark could celebrate a different rags-to-riches story, even one that attributes redemption to faith in God, so long as it doesn't involve someone who also happens to support Donald Trump. Regardless, his political biases explain his scripted reporting of a recent news story. On the 57th anniversary of the iconic and eternally profound Martin Luther King "I Have a Dream" speech, a march was planned by a Leftist group that was also protesting the police shooting of a wanted felon in Wisconsin, Jacob Blake. Blake was shot while resisting arrest on a felony warrant for sexual assault, domestic violence and trespassing, and climbing into a car with his three young children. The resulting riots literally led to massive fires, destruction and some deaths in Kenosha, Wisconsin where the crimes and subsequent shooting occurred. Nationally, similar protests are becoming increasingly violent as the 2020 presidential election nears, with people being injured and killed, police being disobeyed and attacked, and businesses being ransacked and, sometimes, burned to the ground.

Just as described above regarding the July 19, 2020, Pro Police Rally, the police on the ground are being prevented by their superiors from enforcing the law and ending the chaos. Democrat officials, like Mayor Ted Wheeler of Portland, Oregon, who chose to move rather than stop the protestors he coddles and supports from attacking the home he owns, are refusing presidential offers of a prompt resolution through federal assistance. The results of these policies locally are documented in an upcoming film called *Denver in Decay*[17] from Denver radio fixture and filmmaker Steffan Tubbs scheduled for release on September 17, 2020.

As a result, citizens are organizing all around the country, including here in Colorado, to protect life and property, and to stand resolutely and, if needed, forcefully against the violence. One such organizer is Colorado native and Marine John "Tig" Tiegen, a survivor and hero of the 13 Hours in Benghazi and a security and use of force expert. Tiegen put out a call for citizens to make themselves available for the Jacob Blake protest and be ready if the leftist mob was, again, intent on mayhem. In reporting the story on "Next" the night of the affair, Clark took great pains to describe Denver's "peaceful protests" during the day (the destruction almost always comes after dark) before quoting a protest organizer, who was warning people to go home because of "potential right-wing violence in the streets tonight." These were not Clark's words as he was quoting another. But he provided no context for why military heroes might organize with other citizens to, as Tig described it, "protect what's OURS!"

It's perfect, if you're a leftist: devious, subtle, effective. The hero becomes the bad guy for anyone who is not paying attention. Your local news anchor, hard at work.

We must become more proactive and interactive with our media if we don't want to one day soon find ourselves living in a 21st Century, real-life version of George Orwell's prophetic *1984*. Make some noise. Think it through before you do so it is much more than just noise. Letters to the editor, emails and social media posts that point out hypocrisy, bias and falsehoods, and speaking powerfully through your own circles of influence are critical. A fair and honest media, or at least adequate competitive and citizen voices to expose the biases and outright falsehoods of "the other side," are some of the most important mechanisms a free society has with which to hold their government accountable.

The story of Colorado's Corrupt Coordinated Democrat Media Machine driving the leftist agenda to election day and beyond warrants a book of its own. With only a chapter here, I have provided you with some examples that I hope will, at the very least, remind you to assess the biases of the news sources you rely upon and, hopefully, to think about your own:

- What assumptions are you making when you take a news story you read or hear at face value?
- Should you get on your computer and take a look around for some additional or competing information or perspective?
- Did the story you're formulating an opinion around or relying upon for a decision you might make, like voting!, omit key facts or lack significant context?
- Were some of those smooth, seemingly benign words or phrases like "unsubstantiated" allegations or "dueling rallies" slipped in to change your perception of events?
- Did the smiling news anchor selectively quote a leftist "fearing" "right-wing violence in the streets" but not tell you that the citizen defenders organized only <u>after</u> our Queen City, and some of her citizens, had been beaten to a pulp, repeatedly, for months?

- What will you effectively do to counteract it and to encourage others to do the same?

One can never go wrong leaving with quotes from former President Ronald Reagan who, during National Library Week in 1981, said, "If we are to guard against ignorance and remain free, as Jefferson cautioned, it is the responsibility of every American to be informed." Long before that, in 1964, in his prophetic and must-watch "A Time for Choosing"[18] speech, then Hollywood actor Ronald Reagan reminded us that "(t)he trouble with our liberal friends is not that they're ignorant, it's that they know so much that isn't so." The seemingly innate desire of concerned citizens to be accurately informed is an essential trait to the maintenance of a civil society, and one that is being hyper-utilized by the Corrupt Coordinated Democrat Media Machine to flood us with *IN*accurate, often misleading information.

It's happening 24 hours every day because the inmates have, in fact, taken over the asylum. We let it happen. But, it's not too late for our precious Colorado. Get involved. Do your work. Recruit others to help spread the word. Vote like the future of our state is depending on you, *because it is*. And, from this moment forward, *believe nothing you hear and only one-half that you see*.

NOTES

1. Poe, Edgar Allen. The System of Dr. Tarr and Professor Fether
http://pinkmonkey.com/dl/library1/tarr.pdf

2. Colorado COVID-19 Data. Colorado State Emergency Operations Center
https://covid19.colorado.gov/data

3. Schrager, Adam and Witwer, Rob. *The Blueprint – How the Democrats Won Colorado and Why Republicans Everywhere Should Care*. Published May 2010
https://www.ipgbook.com/the-blueprint-products-9781936218004.php?page_id=21

4. Web Site AllSides – *Don't be fooled by media bias and fake news.*
https://www.allsides.com/media-bias/media-bias-chart

5. Paranzino, Mike. *Stop calling it the "Mainstream Media"* RedState.com
https://www.redstate.com/diary/mikeparanzino/2012/03/09/stop-calling-it-the-mainstream-media/

6. Saad, Lydia. *U. S. Still Leans Conservative, but Liberals Keep Recent Gains* Gallup. January 8l, 2019
https://news.gallup.com/poll/245813/leans-conservative-liberals-keep-recent-gains.aspx

7. Send Email to Randy Corporon
wakeupradio2014@gmail.com

8. Tatum, Christine. *In Denver, Residents Lament the Closing of a Newspaper.* The New York Times. March 1, 2009 (The Rocky – closed for good).
https://www.nytimes.com/2009/03/02/business/media/02denver.html?_r=0

9. YouTube *"Good People On Both Sides" Lie Debunked*
https://www.youtube.com/watch?v=rEzcxBn3hbo

10. Heritage Foundation. *A Sampling of Recent Election Fraud Cases from Across the United States*
https://www.heritage.org/voterfraud

11. Bialosky, Bruce. *The Stupidity of Ballot Harvesting and How It Steals Elections.* Townhall February 10, 2019
https://townhall.com/columnists/brucebialosky/2019/02/10/the-stupidity-of-ballot-harvesting-and-how-it-steals-elections-n2540993

12. Roff, Peter. *Al Franken May Have Won His Senate Seat Through Voter Fraud.* USNews July 20, 2010
https://www.usnews.com/opinion/blogs/peter-roff/2010/07/20/al-franken-may-have-won-his-senate-seat-through-voter-fraud

13. Rapp, Nicolas and Jenkins, Aric. *Chart: These 6 Companies Control Much of U.S. Media.* Fortune July 24, 2018 (Comcast, AT&T, Disney, 21st Century Fox, CBS, Cable/Satellite Channels)
https://fortune.com/longform/media-company-ownership-consolidation/

14. Lotz, Ashley *These 6 Corporations Control 90% of The Media in America.* Business Insider June 14, 2012
https://www.businessinsider.com/these-6-corporations-control-90-of-the-media-in-america-2012-6?op=1

15. Frank, John. *How Colorado Republicans transformed from "Never trump" to Donald Trump loyalists in four years.* ColoradoSun. August, 25, 2020
https://coloradosun.com/2020/08/25/colorado-donald-trump-republican-national-convention-never-trump/?utm_source=ActiveCampaign&utm_medium=email&utm_content=Smoke+or+COVID-19%3F+%2F+Colorado+s+%22Never+Trumpers%22+have+changed+%2F+Hunt+for+lost+students+%2F+Rebirth+of+the+ski+bum&utm_campaign=Sunriser+-+8%2F26%2F2020&vgo_ee=v9hSUI9wzChDHtH%2BUT%2FaQXwFoqDlMHNmyq65fGLdufk%3D

16. Osburn, Madeline. *Media Freaks Out On "My Pillow" CEO Mike Lindell For Encouraging Americans To Read the Bible.* TheFederalist March 31, 2020
https://thefederalist.com/2020/03/31/media-freaks-out-on-mypillow-ceo-mike-lindell-for-encouraging-americans-to-read-the-bible/

17. Movie Coming September 17th. *Denver In Decay.* A Steffan Tubbs Film.
http://denverindecay.com/

18. Video A Time for Choosing by Ronald Reagan posted April 2, 2009 recorded October 27, 1964
[1]https://www.youtube.com/watch?v=qXBswFfh6AY

15

FROM BLUEPRINT TO BREAKOUT: COLORADO'S DOWNHILL ROAD TO A CALIFORNIA DYSTOPIA

BY CHARLES HEATHERLY
Political Strategist

In reviewing the dramatic events and sharp controversies of 2020, many will be reminded of the opening lines in Charles Dickens's epic novel, *A Tale of Two Cities.* The story is set in the chaos surrounding the French Revolution, a period of dramatic upheaval, social divisions and organized violence:

"*It was the best of times, it was the worst of times, it was the age of wisdom, it was the age of foolishness, it was the epoch of belief, it was the epoch of incredulity, it was the season of Light, it was the season of Darkness . . .*"

The two contrasting cities in Dickens' famous novel were revolutionary Paris and sober London, but in 2020, our own "season of Light and season of Darkness" are occurring *simultaneously in the same city*, Denver, home to over 700,000 Coloradans and site of the State Capitol, where a ruinous Democrat majority rules without visible regret over violations of the state Constitution. There is Denver the city of Light as celebrated by the Mayor, the city council, the region's major media, and the Capitol's controlling political party – our progressive Democrats. And then, there is Denver the city of Darkness experienced by the residents and victims of the 2020's pandemic – street violence and rapidly rising crime rates.

Our season of Darkness in 2020 is this: In Denver – and dozens of large cities across America – the rule of law and the protection of basic, constitutional freedoms are under assault by an ideological force unprecedented in both scope and intensity.

The breakdown in law enforcement is the common denominator of the two worlds living in uneasy coexistence in Denver. To understand what is happening in the breakdown in law enforcement -- in Denver and in cities controlled for decades by Democrats – one must understand the inherent logic and ideology behind the congenital resistance to any effective crackdown on leftist "street violence." The political program of Progressivism is both a product and a prisoner of its roots in that fountainhead of leftist "idealism," the French Revolution.

You doubt this? Then read a little history, and by that, I mean actual history before Marxists rewrite it to serve partisan groupthink. Coloradans, and especially elected officials obligated to both administer and enforce the law, should understand that most of our "homegrown" Progressives, whether in Denver, Boulder, Aurora or Carbondale, adhere to the socialist maxim, "no enemies to the left." In the Progressives' heart of hearts, the problem to be addressed is not leftist street violence against property, monuments, institutions or people. To the radicals and their Progressive enablers, it is always *resistance* to leftist "social justice" goals and demands that causes the violence.

In the 1928 classic, *The French Revolution: A Monarchist History*, Pierre Gaxotte describes the inescapable logic of revolutionary "progress":

> "*The revolutionary period was characterized by allowing successive avant-garde parties or factions to take political power while riots and disturbances in the streets dictated the actual government policies that were adopted. Against the royal court and the privileged classes, the members of the National Assembly appealed to the turbulent sectors of the capital. Even while privately deploring the excesses committed from July 13 on, they closed their eyes to them because they wanted to hold in reserve the power of the clubs and of the streets. Thus they became prisoners of the alliance they had made; they became prisoners of the formula "no enemies to the left" (pas d'ennemis à gauche).*[1]

Why is our country so deeply divided? The left by its very nature and psychological DNA must *always* sow division as a means of destabilizing the status quo. There is always a new "Popular Front" coalition designed to undermine the pillars of "bourgeois democracy," or in 2020, "systemic racism," in order to advance a radical, "transformative" policy agenda. Unfortunately for the rest of humanity, the targeted "pillars of oppression" turn out to be, well, things like property rights, freedom of speech, freedom of assembly, and freedom of religion. You know, that constitution thing.

In this quadrennial presidential election year, those vivid, warring contrasts in both perceptions and perspectives are visible on the national political scene as well, with citizens' optimistic or pessimistic outlooks a function mainly of their preferred sources of reliable information and their partisan loyalties. They inhabit the same planet, but only barely.

Like the radically different atmospheres in London and Paris at the end of the 18th Century, our nation is deeply divided. The parallels are imperfect but nonetheless striking. In England during and following the French Revolution, conservative parliamentarian Edmund Burke praised the American Revolution and warned of the odor of tyranny seeping from the baskets under French guillotines. Today, the intellectual heirs of the French totalitarians, our academic soothsayers and urban street mobs, bemoan the American Constitution of 1787 as corrupt and, of course, irredeemably "racist."

As Charles Dickens' 18th and 19th Century divisions and contrasts were as much cultural as political, our divisions are only superficially political; they are also deeply cultural and ideological. Leaders in politics, business, science and philanthropy who deny that reality are whistling past the graveyard.

The ruling party in 2020, Colorado's self-styled "progressive Democrats," are celebrating and maximizing autocratic rule through unilateral executive orders and elitist "science-based" commands. In contrast, ordinary working folk, not privy to the magic rings of radical socialism, "intersectionality" and identity politics, stubbornly insist on asking sensible questions challenging the unparalleled arrogance and insatiable political appetites of the centurions and shock troops of "Social Justice." But where did those radical, increasingly costly, inherently insatiable political appetites come from if not from our richly cultivated cultural gardens, our public schools and hallowed institutions of "higher learning"?

Most troubling of all the features of this indigestible and unstable-by-design "New Normal," welcomed and openly institutionalize by Colorado's multimillionaire Governor, is the open complicity and proud partnership of the mainline news media, both print and digital. This semi-paradoxical phenomenon is described in embarrassing detail by this volume's Chapter 14, "Activist Media Protects the Mob."

The "mob" is an apt term for the Antifa provocateurs and street thugs rampaging, looting and disfiguring both public and private property, but it is also an apt metaphor for a governing elite which takes pride in a disdain for constitutional limits to the powers of government. Madison and Hamilton had a more polite term for them in *The Federalist Papers*, "faction," defined as groups seeking private advantage over the common good. But the effect is the same: to our nation's founding generation, federalist and anti-federalist alike, a lawless government is an *illegitimate government*. It remains so in the view of most Americans, the prevailing media whitewash notwithstanding.

The root political problem for most Coloradans is this: the goals of radical social engineering within the radical Progressives' political agenda are inherently hostile and corrosive to the traditional values and institutions of constitutional liberty. This is becoming more apparent each day as the radicals become both more comfortable in laying out their "transformative" agenda and more resistant to law enforcement actions against their street mob allies.

How did this happen? What happened to "Colorado values" as a pillar of stability and civic virtue?

Colorado's journey into incipient lawlessness had its modern regeneration in an ambitious project designed and led by a group of Progressive multimillionaires, the so-called "Gang of Four," originating in a series of private conversations starting around 2002. Their long-range plan for taking control of Colorado government — and it was indeed a multifaceted plan and not merely a goal — was described in considerable detail in a book published in 2010, *The Blueprint*, written by a State Representative, attorney Rob Witwer and his coauthor, journalist Adam Schrager.[2]

Although not especially secretive, the Progressives' ambitious takeover plan for Colorado was not known to the general public until June of 2008, when national conservative columnist Fred Barnes wrote about it in *The Weekly Standard*. The Colorado Model was being implemented but had not yet achieved many of its most important policy goals. That point has not been well understood by Republican leaders and analysts, and the reason for that illustrates a Republican blind spot.

News flash: by 2008, when the Progressives' "Colorado Model" first came to public attention, Colorado Democrats already enjoyed "trifecta" control of Colorado state government. For four years, from the 2007 legislative session through the 2010 session, the state had a Democrat governor, Bill Ritter, and both houses of the legislature had Democrat majorities. That total control of the state was one of the attractions that brought the Democrat National Convention to Denver in 2008. The leaders behind the "Colorado Model" were proud of their achievements, but not yet crowing of major accomplishments at a public panel describing the plan held during what came to be called, the "Obama Convention."

Despite the July national magazine column exposing the ambitious plan and the public panel at the Denver convention, Republican leaders in Colorado took little notice. That's why the Rob Witwer book, *The Blueprint*, made quite a splash when published eighteen months later in 2010. Most Republican strategists had essentially forgotten all about the Colorado Model until the *The Blueprint* arrived like a thunderbolt.

However, as insightful and informative as *The Blueprint* was and is, for many years Republicans misunderstood one key element of the Progressives' strategy. Yes, the "Gang of Four" and their team prioritized *winning above fratricidal infighting:* they stressed *unity and victory* above ideological purity in building successful coalition campaigns. Many Republican strategists did in fact begin emphasizing unity and winning above narrow factionalism. But that priority has been widely misunderstood.

The Progressives' priority for winning through coalition politics was a *campaign tactic,* a basic political necessity, not an abandonment of radical, collectivist, essentially socialist policy goals. When all was said and done, from 2002 to 2008 and beyond, the decision-making strategists sitting around the table plotting the next election campaign *were all Progressives.* Their agenda was the Obama agenda and the Saul Alinsky agenda. There were no "blue dog Democrats" in those planning sessions. Their policy agenda was tactically pragmatic but at bottom very radical.

Colorado Progressives embraced President Obama's radical vision of a "*transformative agenda*," which would "redeem America" in the eyes of radicals the world over. Jimmy Carter? Bill Clinton? Hell no! They were history: These new Colorado Democrat leaders were cut from a different cloth; they were real mountain-plains radical progressives, not southern state wannabes.

To put it more graphically, neither Jimmy Carter nor Bill Clinton – both former Southern state governors – could win a Democrat presidential primary in Colorado today.

To "cut to the chase," that is why the Democrat "trifecta" elected in 2018 – led by one of their own, Governor Jared Polis – is a different breed of political animal than prior Democrat majorities in the legislature. The Democrat majorities in the legislature from 2007 through 2010 and 2013-14 were liberal to be sure, but they were not yet committed to a truly radical, broad "transformative" policy agenda. By the time the 2019 "trifecta" took power, Progressives were ready to rock 'n roll; and roll they did.

Another feature of the "Colorado Model" misunderstood in the Republicans' rendering of Democrat coalition plans in *The Blueprint* -- and thus underestimated in importance by Republicans generally-- was a key building block of the Progressives winning strategy: generous investments in creating, growing and nurturing a large network of non-profit organizations *outside the Democrat Party structure.* That network of federally chartered 501(c)3 and 501(c)4 non-profits cannot participate directly in election campaigns, but they can and do grow lists and legions of policy advocates. Their cultural infrastructure works tirelessly to generate public support for Progressives' radical policy agenda.

Republicans in 2010 lacked anything remotely resembling that infrastructure network with an ideological commitment to the progressive worldview and matching policy agenda. Republican leaders on the whole lacked any interest in or commitment to creating a parallel civic infrastructure.

The "Californication" of Colorado politics and government continues in 2020 -- and at an accelerating pace. Having lived and worked in California for twenty years, this author witnessed first-hand that state's downhill slide into a socialist stupor. A principal "precipitating factor" in that decline was fratricide among Republicans in response to election losses. When Republicans enjoy "circular firing squads" more than confronting and defeating radical legislation, it's time to reboot.

The authors of UNMASKED2020 offer a dozen chronicles of progressive policy failures in a year of escalating street violence, unprecedented economic dislocations, and of course, "social distancing." The social distancing that most needs to occur is the abandonment of failed leadership.

- Chapter 9 describes the Democrats' cram-down of a "tax reform" bill that essentially kicked our state's economic recovery to the curb.
- Capitol security and our Governor were AWOL while mobs of Antifa-led hooligans broke windows and defaced the State Capitol with obscene political graffiti.

- The Governor took advantage of public health emergency powers to shackle small business, drive up unemployment to over 300,000, and foster a $3.3 billion loss of state revenues – all in order to fight a virus which has a mortality rate (or "Infection Fatality Rate") of below 1% for the Colorado population as a whole (.0065 according to a July 15 CDC report).[3]
- For the first time in history, government ordered a quarantine of millions of healthy people, not the individuals most afflicted. Not only was the coronavirus "novel," so was government's inchoate, ruinous response.
- In the last three weeks of the 2020 legislative session, 46 new Democrat-sponsored bills were introduced on top of the 546 already processed — and 42 budget-related bills — many with expensive price tags, violating promises made to minority Republicans and business organizations, and with public involvement in committee hearings severely restricted.
- For the first time in Colorado history, the hours of legislative business at the Capitol were restricted out of an acknowledged fear of violence after dark — and the admission by law enforcement agencies (including the agency accountable to the Governor) that they could not protect lawmakers after they left the building.
- A Senator from rural Larimer County confirms that the radical Democrats now in control of the legislature are *different*; in 2020, one-party-control of government has more profound — and possibly irreversible-- consequences than it did in past generations.

Colorado's experiment with radical progressivism has failed; only the colorful facade remains, a facade propped up by an activist, biased media striving unapologetically to be on "the right side of history" (of course, that is a pretty low standard if Marxists are writing the history books). In the meantime, ranchers, construction workers, restaurant workers, insurance brokers, law enforcement officers and most taxpayers may well look upon the radicals' echo chamber antics quite differently when asked to support such orchestrated chaos at the ballot box.

Some readers may think the "season of Light and season of Darkness" metaphor is overdrawn; after all, we are constantly told that the radicals are "idealistic" and have "good intentions." But, what are those "ideals" and "good intentions?" Voters as well as consumers should remember to always read the fine print on the contract. It is fair to wonder: Was Governor Polis thinking only of the common good when he waited almost two full months before having a 6-foot fence erected all around the State Capitol to protect it from ongoing nightly attacks while repairs were underway? The estimated costs of the repairs at the Capitol are suspiciously an ever-changing (and secret) figure in the hands of the governor's appointees at the Department of Personnel and Administration.

The Bible offers ageless wisdom on this matter. *I Thessalonians 5:21* tells us, "*test all things; hold fast that which is good.*" That is a counsel of prudence, a virtue lost on too many crusaders chasing their page in history. Yet, history is a hard taskmaster. Our history books include not only the "Dark Ages" but a hundred million deaths in the 20th Century at the hands of communist dictators.

Ronald Reagan often remarked that he hesitated to ask God to be on his side; he worried more about being on God's side. Let's beware the Mandarins of historical benevolence.

We cannot control whether we find ourselves in a season of Light or a season of Darkness. But we can, as the Bible advises, choose to "*hold fast that which is good*."

NOTES

1. Cited by Kenneth D. Whitehead, "No Enemies to the Left," in the *New Oxford Review* https://www.newoxfordreview.org/documents/no-enemies-to-the-left-still/

1. Schrager, Adam and Witwer, Rob. *The Blueprint – How the Democrats Won Colorado and why Republicans Everywhere Should Care.* Fulcrum Publishing, 2010.
Also at IPGBook.com
https://fulcrum.bookstore.ipgbook.com/the-blueprint-products-

3. CDC Report. July 15, 2020
https://www.cdc.gov/coronavirus/2019-ncov/hcp/planning-scenarios.html

BIOGRAPHIES – AUTHORS

John Andrews has been president of the Colorado Senate, Republican nominee for Governor, the original host of Backbone Radio, and chairman of the Western Conservative Summit. He helped found the Independence Institute in 1985, the State Policy Network in 1992, the Republican Study and the Centennial Institute in 2009. He is the author of Responsibility Reborn and the editor of BackboneAmerica.net.

Gray Buckley, BS, MPA, was a 9-1-1 dispatcher; instructed at The American University and at the University of Colorado; and was a Maryland State Police trooper in patrol, investigations, and headquarters staff. He helped organize the Lakewood CO police before joining the Colorado Bureau of Investigation to lead the Organized Crime Intelligence Program, and criminal identification and information services. He chaired the FBI's National Crime Information Center Advisory Policy Board and did similar work for the U.S. Department of Homeland Security. He is past president of the Retired Peace Officers of Colorado.

Born in Denver, **Randy Corporon** opened and ran a multi-location High Performance Classic Car Auto Repair and Paint business before enrolling and graduating from the Ron Bailey School of Broadcasting. He graduated from Colorado College in 1995 with a BA in English, and soon enrolled in the University of Denver Sturm College of Law. After graduating law school and passing the bar exam, he opened his private law practice in 1998. Besides leading a flourishing law practice, Corporon hosts a Saturday morning radio talk show on 710KNUS and is now serving a two-year term as Colorado's Republican National Committeeman.

Karl Dierenbach has been an engineer for Ford Motor Company and a patent attorney in Denver. Throughout his engineering and legal careers he was constantly developing and evaluating cutting edge technologies. Now Karl employs his skills to write about technological, political and cultural issues for various outlets. He is an unapologetic conservative who has written and researched for political causes and campaigns. Karl lives south of Denver, Colorado, with his wonderful wife and three amazing sons.

Charles Heatherly earned a B.A. at the University of Arizona and an M.A. in American Government at the Claremont Graduate University. In 1980 he was editor of the Heritage Foundation's landmark MANDATE FOR LEADERSHIP blueprint and later a Reagan presidential appointee in two federal agencies. In 2002 he arrived in Colorado as staff to Congressman Tom Tancredo before moving to the Colorado General Assembly in 2010 as Director of Policy and Strategic Initiatives for the Senate Republican caucus. In 2020 he was principal budget analyst for the House Minority Caucus.

Born and raised in Colorado, **Jeff Hunt** is the leader of a Colorado think-tank. He is also the organizer of one of the largest gatherings of conservatives in the Western United States, hosting Donald Trump, Phil Robertson, Dr. Ben Carson, Sarah Palin, and many others. He has previously served on the Presidential campaigns for Rick Santorum and Mitt Romney. He was the founder of Avinova Media Group and Director of Operations for the Clapham Group. He is an ultra-marathoner and adventurer. He spent five summers as a river guide in Buena Vista, CO. He and his wife have four children and can often be found enjoying Colorado state parks.

Patricia Kurgan is the founder and CEO of Astro Logistics, Inc., a business consulting and transportation logistics firm, and is research director for The Kim Monson Show on 560KLZ Radio. Kurgan has extensive involvement with business enterprises, community boards and elected public officials on public policy issues affecting local communities. She served from 2010-2012 as a member of the state Pay Equity Commission and has testified often on behalf of small business owners and community concerns in numerous legislative hearings.

Kevin Lundberg was a member of the Colorado legislature from 2003 to 2018. He continues in the political arena including as the executive director for the Republican Study Committee of Colorado. Kevin lives with his wife Sandy in Larimer County, just west of Berthoud. Kevin and Sandy helped start Christian Home Educators of Colorado in 1990 and he served on their board of trustees from 1990 to 2018. He is also an Institute Fellow for the Centennial Institute and a trustee for Colorado Christian University.

Kim Monson is the host of two radio shows that air in the Denver Metro and Colorado markets. The Kim Monson Show which broadcasts on KLZ 560 AM focuses on news, politics and opinion by looking at the issues as "Freedom vs Force, Force vs Freedom." Kim Monson brings our Veteran's stories alive on America's Veteran's Stories which airs on EZ 1430 AM in the Denver market. She has interviewed over 140 WWII Veterans and Veterans of our other wars and conflicts. Kim is the recipient of the 2020 Vern Bickel Award for Grass Roots Leadership from the Independence Institute. She is also the recipient of the 2016 Leadership Program of the Rockies Leader in Action Award. Kim Monson served on the Lone Tree, Colorado City Council, 2012-2016.

Kim Ransom was elected to the Colorado State Legislature in 2014, and currently serves on the Joint Budget Committee as the sole House Republican. Prior to serving on the JBC, Kim was appointed to a number of Committees, including Health, Insurance & Environment; Transportation & Local Government; Education; and Public Health. A former high school teacher, Kim has studied and taught the Constitution. She has lived in her District since 1986, and raised her four children in Douglas County. While they were growing up, she was involved in their schools, sports activities, childrens' theater productions, and their church. Now grown, they are all successful adults that make their mother quite proud.

Paul Seby is a leading practitioner of law in the Rocky Mountain region, with nearly 25 years' experience analyzing a myriad of environmental issues. Seby has vast experience prosecuting cases to enforce and overturn administrative agency regulations and decisions, and has defended clients in federal and state enforcement proceedings in appearances before the U.S. Supreme Court, U.S. Courts of Appeal, and the Colorado Supreme Court, among others. Clients across the country trust Paul Seby to draw upon his deep understanding of how government programs and agencies function to identify existing and potential environmental pitfalls they may face in achieving their business goals.

Kelly Sloan was born and raised in Calgary Alberta, Canada, and graduated from Mount Royal University with a degree in Criminology. He moved to Colorado in 2006 with the energy industry and started his own public affairs and communications firm in 2010, representing a variety of clients at the state legislature and in Washington, D.C. He is a policy fellow at the Centennial Institute and writes regular columns for *Colorado Politics* and *The Washington Examiner.* He has been published in several statewide and national publications, and he has been a guest commentator on local, regional, and national radio and television.

Senator **Jerry Sonnenberg** is a farmer and rancher from Sterling. He has served in the Colorado Legislature since 2007, starting in the House of Representatives and moving into the Senate in 2015. His senate district (District 1) covers most of Northeastern Colorado. Jerry has served as Senate Pro Tempore and chair of the Agriculture and Natural Resources Committee and continues to be the go to legislative expert in water resources and agricultural interests.

Dave Williams is often described as one of the most effective and aggressive representatives in the Colorado legislature. The first Latino elected to represent El Paso County's House District 15 in 2016, Williams serves on the House Business Affairs and Labor Committee and the Committee on State, Veterans and Military Affairs. Currently Vice-President of Logistics for a manufacturing support services company, he has served in several leadership capacities in both small business and local politics. In the 2020 legislative session he was the House Republican floor leader for the debate on the $30 billion state budget bill.

Rob Woodward is a state senator in Colorado. He was elected to the Colorado General Assembly as a Republican in November 2018. Senator Woodward represents Senate District 15 which encompasses most of Larimer County outside of Fort Collins. He and his wife, Paula, have been married since 1991, and have three children: Andrew, Allie and Kate. Senator Woodward owns 28 Subway franchises in Northern Colorado, Wyoming and Nebraska,[i] and manages over 450 employees. He opened his first store at the age of 21.

APPENDIX A – EXECUTIVE ORDERS BY GOVERNOR POLIS

LINK TO GOVERNOR'S WEB PAGE
https://www.colorado.gov/governor/2020-executive-orders

As of September 2, 2020 Governor Polis has issued 176 'D' Executive Orders. (2019 data unavailable)
John Hickenlooper – Governor – 2011-2018
Jared Polis – Governor – 2019 - present

Examples – 2020 Orders

March 11, 2020
D 2020-003 Declaring a Disaster Emergency Due to the Presence of Coronavirus disease 2019 in Colorado

March 18, 2020
D 2020-007 Ordering Suspension of Normal In-Person Instruction at All Public and Private Elementary and Secondary Schools in the State of Colorado Due to the

Presence of COVID-19

March 19, 2020
D 2020-009 Ordering the Temporary Cessation of All Elective and Non-Essential Surgeries and Procedures and Preserving Personal Protective Equipment and Ventilators in Colorado Due to the Presence of COVID-19

March 25, 2020
D 2020-017 Ordering Coloradans to Stay at Home Due to the Presence of COVID-19 in the State

April 17, 2020
D 2020-039 Ordering Workers in Critical Businesses and Critical Government Functions to Wear Non-Medical Face Coverings

April 26, 2020
D 2020-044 Safer at Home

April 26, 2020
B 2020-002 Creating the Governor's New Normal Advisory Board

May 16, 2020
D 2020-067 Extending Executive Order D 2020 039 Ordering Workers in Critical Businesses and Critical Government Functions to Wear Non-Medical Face Coverings

June 1, 2020
D 2020-091 Safer at Home and in the Vast, Great Outdoors

June 30, 2020
D 2020-123 Amending and Extending Executive Order D 2020 091 Safer at Home and in the Vast, Great Outdoors

July 9, 2020
D 2020-127 Protect Our Neighbors

July 23, 2020
D 2020-144 Amending and Extending Executive Orders D 2020 091, D 2020 123, and D 2020 142 Safer at Home and in the Vast, Great Outdoors

July 23, 2020
D 2020 – 145 Extending Executive Orders D 2020 045, D 2020 080, and D 2020 114 Permitting the Limited Recommencement of Voluntary or Elective Surgeries and Procedures in Colorado

August 14, 2020
D 2020-164 Amending and Extending Executive Orders D 2020 039, D 2020 067, D 2020 092, D 2020 110, and D 2020 138 Ordering Individuals in Colorado to Wear Non-Medical Face Coverings

August 21, 2020
D 2020-170 Amending and Extending Executive Orders D 2020 091, D 2020 123, D 2020 142, and D 2020 144 Safer at Home and in the Vast, Great Outdoors

August 24, 2020
D 2020-172 Extending Executive Orders D 2020 014, D 2020 028, D 2020 048, D 2020 083, D 2020 117, and D 2020 146

Concerning the Temporary Suspension of Certain Requirements Preventing Issuance of Marriage Licenses Due to the Presence of COVID-19 in Colorado

September 2, 2020
D 2020-176 Extending Executive Orders D 2020 003, D 2020 018, D 2020 032, D 2020 058, D 2020 076, D 2020 109, D 2020 125, and D 2020 152 Declaring a Disaster Emergency Due to the Presence of Coronavirus Disease 2019 in Colorado (expires 30 days from September 2, 2020)

September 6, 2020
D 2020-179 Amending and Extending Executive Orders D 2020 005, D 2020 008, D 2020 036, D 2020 061, D 2020 095, D 2020 129, and D 2020 155 Concerning Limiting In-Person Contact for the 2020 Elections and the Secretary of State's Operations Due to the Presence of COVID-19 in Colorado

ADDITIONAL INFORMATION

Public Health Order 20-24 (Stay at Home) and 20-22 (Closing Certain Businesses)

Both orders aim to limit the spread of COVID-19 by minimizing contact between people. Closing Certain Businesses (20-22) closed bars, restaurants, gyms and similar facilities so large groups of people do not gather. Stay-at-Home (20-24) further limits contact by ordering all Coloradans to stay at home unless they are engaged in certain necessary activities. Please refer to the public health orders themselves for a detailed list of what is allowed and disallowed. Businesses that have questions should read the orders carefully and consult an attorney if unable to determine how their business fits in.

More information on Colorado Department of Public Health and Environment Web Page https://covid19.colorado.gov/stay-home-except-essential-needs

This information accessed September 8, 2020

APPENDIX B
RESOURCES & RECOMMENDED READING

I. Dimensions of the 2020 COVID-19 Pandemic

What you need to know about the CARES Act, Alliance Defending Freedom, https://uploads-ssl.webflow.com/5a4d1738e77d7900016a366c/5e8f3be0b36f973fb9b51042_ADF%20-%205%20thing%20to%20know-CARES%20Act.pdf

John Tierney, *The Politics of Fear*, CITY JOURNAL, May 20,2020.

Joel Kotkin, *The Pandemic Road to Serfdom,* TheAmericanMind.org, May 5, 2020.

Victor Davis Hanson, *The Thin Facade of Authority (Botched Models, Bad Advice)*, American Greatness, April 12, 2020.

Peter Earle, *Coronavirus and Disease Modeling*, American Institute for Economic Research, 2020. https://www.amazon.com/dp/1630692115/ref=rdr_ext_tmb

Antony Davies and James R. Harrigan, *The COVID-19 Catastrophe, American Institute for Economic Research,* https://www.statnews.com/2020/03/17/a-fiasco-in-the-making-as-the-coronavirus-pandemic-takes-hold-we-are-making-decisions-without-reliable-data/

Michael Barone, *Were the Lockdowns a Mistake?* Real Clear Politics, September 4, 2020.

John Ioannidis, *A Fiasco in the Making,* Stanford University,

STATNEWS, *https://www.statnews.com/2020/03/17/a-fiasco-in-the-making-as-the-coronavirus-pandemic-takes-hold-we-are-making-decisions-without-reliable-data/*

Barry Bronstein, *The Tyranny of (Alleged) Experts*, American Institute for Economic Research, 2020.

Centers for Disease Control, *COVID-19 Pandemic Planning Scenarios*, July 15, 2020

NCSL, *Balancing Legislative and Executive Powers in Emergencies*, National Council of State Legislatures, July, 2020.

Peter Kolchinsky, *Understanding How [COVID-19] Testing Works*, CITY JOURNAL, April, 2020.

Steven Malanga, *The Crisis's Impact on Budgets*, CITY JOURNAL, March 22,2020.

Centers for Disease Control, *Provisional Death Counts for Coronavirus Disease (COVID-19),* April, 2020.

Brian Patrick Eha, *The Media and the Virus,* CITY JOURNAL, Summer, 2020.

Barry Farah, *Masking freedom, ignoring science*, Coloradopolitics.com, July 22, 2020.

Heather Mac Donald, *Four Months of Unprecedented Government Malfeasance*, IMPRIMIS, Hillsdale College, May-June2020.

Which states are poised for economic recovery after covid-19? AMERICNA LEGISLATIVE EXCHANGE COUNCIL, *https://www.alec.org/*

Jessica Seaman, "Colorado to declare racism a public health crisis after a push by agency staff to respond to protests, pandemic," *The Denver Post,* July 31, 2020.

II. Politics, Economics, Civic Discourse & Elections

Will Lloyd, *Michael Anton and the Strakes in the 2020 election*, THE SPECTATOR, *https://spectator.us/michael-anton-stakes-2020-election/*

Voting is Not Going to Be Enough This Year, TRUE THE VOTE, *https://truethevote.org*

Christopher Caldwell, *America Cowering: What Civil Rights Law Has Become*, THE CLAREMONT REVIEW OF BOOKS, Summer 2020,,*https://claremontreviewofbooks.com/america-cowering/*

The anti-racist drive to turn schools into propaganda mills, THE MANHATTAN INSTITUTE, *https://www.manhattan-institute.org/anti-racist-drive-woke-schools-propaganda-mills*

Edward J. Erler, Jr., *The Riot Party: The Left Perfects the Mob Veto*, THE AMERICAN MIND, September, 2020, *https://americanmind.org/essays/the-riot-party/*

The Left Preps for Civil War, PJ MEDIA, September 9, 2020, *https://www.realclearpolitics.com/2020/09/09/left_preps_for_civil_war_potential_for_violent_conflict_is_high_522772.html?utm_source=rcp-today&utm_medium=email&utm_campaign=mailchimp-*

newsletter&mc_cid=d87174ed64&mc_eid=36b1a9d3a5

Matthew J. Peterson, *The Racial Marxism of BLM,* THE AMERICAN MIND, September 1, 2020. https://americanmind.org/features/the-racial-marxism-of-blm/

Mike Gonzalez, *The Revolution Is Upon Us*, LAW &LIBERTY, https://lawliberty.org/the-revolution-is-upon us/?utm_source=LAL+Updates&utm_campaign=8989626964CAL_Daily_Updates&utm_medium=email&utm_term=0_53ee3e1605-8989626964-72442433

F.A. Hayek, *The Road to Serfdom*, University of Chicago Press, 1944.

The 1619 Project: A Critique, by Phillip W. Magness, American Institute for Economic Research, 2020. https://www.amazon.com/dp/1630692018/ref=as_sl_pc_tf_til?tag=aier0b-20&linkCode=w00&linkId=f3a077c6f9d4f715dab10cec3d374e5c&creativeASIN=1630692018

Allen Guelzo, *The 1619 Projects Tells a False Story about Capitalism, Too*, THE WALL STREET JOURNAL, May 8, 2020, https://www.wsj.com/articles/the-1619-project-tells-a-false-story-about-capitalism-too-11588956387

Donald J. Kochan, *What Does Federalist-1 Teach Us about the Importance of Civil Discourse?* https://fedsoc.org/commentary/fedsoc-blog/what-does-federalist-1-teach-us-about-the-importance-of-civil-discourse?

James R. Copland, *The Unelected: How An Unaccountable Elite Is*

Governing America, Encounter Books, 2020.
https://www.amazon.com/Unelected-Unaccountable-Elite-Governing-America/dp/1641771208/?tag=lawliberty-20

Hayden R. Ludwig, *Big Money in Dark Shadows,* Capital Research Center, Washington, D.C., 2020.

Bradley C. S. Watson, *A Politics of Nietzschean Righteousness,* Law and Liberty,
http://lawliberty/book-review/the-recipe-for-a-wrathful-politics/

Williamson Evers, *The Crisis in Civil Rights: Best Books and Articles on Race, Police, and the Welfare State*, Independent Institute, Oakland, California, 2020.

California's Worst Bills of the [2020] Legislative Session, CALIFORNIA POLITICAL REVIEW,
http://www.capoliticalreview.com/top-stories/californias-worst-bills-of-the-legislative-session/

Edward Ring, *California Pushes the Frontiers of Woke*, CALIFONIA POLITICAL REVIEW, June, 2020,
http://www.capoliticalreview.com/top-stories/california-pushes-the-frontiers-of-woke/

San Francisco Museum of Modern Art Is Latest Scene of Cancel Culture, CALIFORIA POLITICAL REVIEW,
http://www.capoliticalreview.com/top-stories/latest-scene-of-cancel-culture-sf-museum-of-modern-art/

Darrell Huff, *How to Lie with Statistics*, W. W. Norton & Company, 1954.

BALLOTPEDIA, https://ballotpedia.org/Main_Page

III. Colorado Government & the 2020 Legislative Session

Office of Legislative Legal Services, *"Scope of Governor's Power to Issue Executive Orders,"* *https://leg.colorado.gov/sites/default/files/scope-of-governors-power-to-issue-executive-orders.pdf*

2020 DIGEST OF BILLS [Summary of 329 bills enacted into law and three bills vetoed in 2020 session] *https://leg.colorado.gov/publications/2020-digest-bills*

Summary of Governor's constitutional and statutory emergency powers, OFFICE OF LEGISLATIVE LEGAL SERVICES, August, 2020, *https://leg.colorado.gov/publications/memorandum-governors-constitutional-and-statutory-emergency-powers*

Colorado Quarterly Economic Forecast of June 2020, Legislative Council Staff, *https://leg.colorado.gov/publications/forecast-june-2020*

The United States Constitution and the Colorado Constitution https://www.sos.state.co.us/pubs/info_center/laws/COConstitution/ColoradoConstitution.pdf

The Declaration of Independence, *https://www.archives.gov/founding-docs/declaration-transcript*

Colorado State Budget, FY2021: *Appropriations Report* [667 pages], *http://leg.colorado.gov/sites/default/files/fy20-21apprept_0.pdf*

Summary of Gov. Polis's Executive Orders issued during the COVID-19 public health

http://leg.colorado.gov/publications/summary-governor%E2%80%99s-executive-orders-issued-during-covid-19-emergency

Summary of federal legislation passed in 2020 in response to COVID-19 http://leg.colorado.gov/publications/updated-summary-federal-legislation-passed-response-covid-19-20-11

Adam Schrager and Rob Witwer, *Blueprint: How the Democrats Won Colorado and why Republicans everywhere should care.* Fulcrum Publishing, May 2010

Nell Salzman, *George Brauchler, Patrick Neville Warn of Coming Crime Wave in Colorado*, WESTWORD, July 6, 2020.

IV. History, Religion & Culture

George Orwell, *1984*, Signet Classics, 1950.

Charles Mackay, *Extraordinary Popular Delusions and Madness of Crowds*, Crown Trade Paperbacks, 1980.

Daron Acemogll and James A. Robinson, *Why Nations Fail: The Origins of Power, Prosperity, and Poverty*, Currency, 2012.

Edmund Burke, *Reflections on the Revolution in France*, Oxford World's Classics.

John M. Ellis, *The Breakdown of Higher Education*, Encounter Books, 2020.

Skousen, W. Cleon. *The 5000 Year Leap: A Miracle That Changed the World,* National Center for Constitutional Studies, 2006.

The Bible, Old and New Testaments.

V. RESOURCES

Alliance Defending Freedom, Scottsdale, Arizona, *ADFlegal.org*

The Independence Institute, Denver, Colorado, *i21.org*

The Heritage Foundation, Washington, D.C., *Heritage.org*

Capital Research Center, Washington, D.C., *capitalresearch.org*

American Institute for Economic Research, Washington, D.C., *aier.org*

True the Vote, Houston, TX, *https://truethevote.org*

American Legislative Exchange Council, Washington, DC., *alec.org*

National Center for State Legislatures, Denver, Colorado, *ncsl.org*

The Federalist Society, Washington, DC. , *fedsoc.org*

The Claremont Institute, Upland, California, *claremont.org*

The Manhattan Institute/ CITY JOURNAL, *manhattan-institute.org*

National Association of Scholars, New York, NY *nas.org*

INDEX

(Number represents Chapter #)

About The Republican Study Committee of Colorado (RSCC)

RSCC.US

Who We Are

The Republican Study Committee of Colorado (RSCC) is an association of elected Colorado Republican legislators who develop and support legislative action consistent with the core values and goals of the Republican Party. We first organized in 2005, after the progressive left took the majorities in both the Colorado House and Senate. As our name suggests, we patterned our group after the Republican Study Committee (RSC) in the U.S. House of Representatives. Soon after organizing we spent several very productive hours consulting with the then chair of the RSC, Mike Pence.

What We Do

- As members of the RSCC, we take principled stands on tough issues, create high standards for developing and evaluating legislation, and vote consistent with the core values of our Party.
- We are committed to in-depth study of critical issues that impact the citizens of Colorado while responding to our constituents' concerns through focused exploration and reasoned debate.
- The RSCC provides long-range planning and continuity between legislative sessions. We foster coordination

with nonprofit groups in advancing conservative issues, and increase state-to-state and national sharing and organization of legislative information.

Where We Stand

We believe the core values and goals of the Republican Party reflect the principles of our nation's Founders, the U.S. Constitution and our Colorado Constitution, and that these values must remain central to all legislation.

Core Values

Protect Individual Liberty

Limit Government

Protect Private Property

National Sovereignty

Enforce Rule of Law

Protect Sanctity of Life

Enforce Legal Immigration

Free Markets and Commerce

Lower Taxes

Support Family Integrity

Deliver Quality Education

Stewardship of Natural Resources

High Quality and Affordable Medical Care

Encourage Faith-based Charities

Personal Responsibility

Made in the USA
Columbia, SC
22 September 2020